Island Voices

Also by Kawau Island Bookworms

An Island Summer

Island Voices

Written by Members of the Kawau Island Bookworms

©Kawau Island Bookworms 2014

All rights reserved. No part of this publication may be reproduced or transmitted in any form or by any means, electronic or mechanical, including scanning, photocopying, recording, or any information storage or retrieval system, without permission in writing from the publisher.

Cover Photography: Ruth E. Henderson

Title Page photo: Ruth E. Henderson

Photos and drawings within stories provided by author.

Additional photos by Ruth E. Henderson

Cover and book design: Stephen Horsley – Outline Design

Woodcuts by Chic Vercoe

Editing and proofing team: Lois E. Hunter, Jane Myhre, Ruth E. Henderson

Layout: Lin Pardey

Printing: ExPress Communications Ltd. Snells Beach

Printed in New Zealand

ISBN: 978-1-9292141-49-5

For information contact Lin Pardey, lpardey@xtra.co.nz Private Bag 906, Victoria St. West, Auckland 1142, New Zealand

Contents

Introduction - Lin Pardey	8
Foreword - Where to Start? - Lynne Banton	11

PART ONE
FICTION

Faces - Chic Vercoe	14
Six Degrees of Separation - Lois E. Hunter	18
Island Time - Lin Pardey	24
Laura - Diane Gray	30
Life is Sweet - Helen Jeffery	42
The Culling - David Kendall	46
Beginning, Middle and End - Lois E. Hunter	50

PART TWO
FACT

How I Came to Kawau - Ruth MacClement	54
The Mail Bag - Lyn Hume	57
I Built This House - Ruth MacClement	60

Kawau - From Then to Now - Gael Archer	62
Toby - Jenny Gibbons	76
I Love Brash Tuis - Ruth MacClement	78
The Dolphins - Ruth MacClement	79
Lessons the Weka Teach - Ruth MacClement	80
A 40 Year Journey to Kawau - Cheryl Hoyle	82
Butterscotch Sun - Ruth MacClement	84
I'll Never Want to Leave Soon - Fay Richardson	86
An Island Love Affair - Lynne Banton	93
Visions to Kawau Reality - Ruth MacClement	100

PART THREE
SOMEWHERE BETWEEN FICTION AND FACT

Snapshots - Ruth E. Henderson	104
Nelson Girls: A Dog's Tale - Jen Seel and Jen Spring	124
Tide Talk - Jane Myhre	130

Introduction

What is a Short Story?

Lin Pardey

The first of the autumn gales roars, rain showers blot out the islands one minute, sunshine glistens off white capped waves the next. Twelve members of the Kawau Island Bookworms are sheltered from this first hint of winter, sharing hot soup, fresh scones and piles of books we've read in the month since our last gathering. "Okay," someone says, "We had lots of fun putting together a progressive novel last winter, what we going to do to stretch our brains this time?"

"Let's each try writing a short story," someone states.

"About island life," chimes in another.

"I'm not a writer, couldn't do it!" Is a comment echoed by three attendees.

The Bookworms is in many ways a unique group. Composed of about two dozen Kawau Island residents, it is informal; just come along to a different home once each month and share whatever you've been reading, have some lunch, catch up with what is happening on other parts of the island. Because there are no roads on this special island, because the population fluctuates by seasons, the number of attendees also tends to fluctuate, with summer meetings often attracting almost two dozen members and extremely stormy winter days cutting that number to six or seven. But no matter the numbers, the lively discussions that arise from talking about the books we each like or dislike has kept this group going and evolving for almost a quarter of a century.

The idea of working on a progressive novel started out as a bit of a lark. But when 17 different people added their ideas, and the resulting light hearted story was turned into a printed book, the reaction was better than anyone had expected, both from participants and readers. Actually holding a printed book in your hand, knowing your name and words are in its pages can be quite thrilling. Those who received or bought copies of the book enjoyed it too. So the idea of a book of short stories , written during those dark hours of winter when you might otherwise be feeling restless or bored, took root immediately. Then the debate began, one that continued through two more monthly gatherings - what exactly is a short story?

    I stated my opinion, "It has a beginning, a middle and an end. Something causes change in a characters life. It is less than 10,000 words."

    "Ten thousand words? I couldn't write 500,"

    "Can it be true or does it have to be fiction to be a short story?"

    "Does it have to be prose? Can it be a poem?"

    "Whatever do I write about?"

    In the nature of the Bookworms Club, the guidelines stayed informal, there were only two rules; the subject - something about island life, and the second , one every editor knows is vital, a deadline. I was given the surprisingly difficult job of deciding the order in which each of the stories should be presented. This was not a simple task as 17 people met that deadline including all three of those who stated they weren't writers. My brief was to arrange these stories so readers would be lead from one story to the next and want to keep reading, writers would feel their work was fully appreciated and finally that some sort of logic prevailed. Three of the submitters were professional writers but their contributions though enjoyable to read, in no way outshine many of the non-professionally written stories so their stories are interspersed with those written by absolute first timers. Fictional short stories, totally factual stories, poems - these were relatively easy to place, but then came three that didn't fit either category. When a dog narrates a story that is a depiction of what its owner does on an island, is it fiction or is it fact? To solve this problem, I made up a third category and called it - *Somewhere Between Fiction and Fact.*

    We hope you enjoy these glimpses of Island life as seen through the eyes of people who live on this special piece of earth, surrounded by water and beset by the special problems this potential isolation entails. I know everyone one of us who participated in this project had to fight to get these words on paper, had doubts about the subject they choose to write about, insecurities about having others judge their words. Each contributor came through with flying colors which should be an inspiration to anyone who has thought, "Someday I'd like to sit down and write about my life."

So what is a short story? Read through this book and you'll probably agree – the definition is as flexible as your imagination.

Where to Start?

Lynne Banton

A story with an island theme, that's what we have to write
Ideas rotate around my head, keeping me awake at night
Should I write a romantic story, with characters from days gone by?
Where would I start, perhaps that's too hard or shall I have a try?

A fishing tale on a stormy sea, a man overboard perhaps
But would it all get too complicated with rescue boats and maps
So how about a romantic tale, cruising atolls and islands abound
I'll have to think up a storyline - could the cruise ship run aground?

Perhaps I could write about an island, far away from any mainland
Palms fringing on the distant shore, smooth rocks and golden sand
But who would be on the island, would they live like castaways?
Too hard to write a story of how they spent their days!

An island murder, that's a good read, where would be the killing spot?
Now I'll have to choose the weapon, who did it and what's the plot?
I'm not cut out as an author; my stories would bore you to the end
A never ending tale...now's the time for me to press send!

Part One

Fiction

Faces

Chic Vercoe

She opened her eyes to bright, warm sunlight then checked her watch for the time. Five past eight!

She couldn't believe that she had slept for so long. Good sleep, uninterrupted sleep, dreamless sleep. She could not stop the tears of relief that arrived as she dared to hope that this was the turning point she had been waiting for. Last night was the third time in the last week that this had happened.

She was into her fifth week of self-imposed exile and sleep had been elusive. Short bursts of two to three hours followed by conversations with her chatty brain, analysing, chastising and worrying herself into fear of the now and the never-never. Getting out of bed, making a cup of tea and reading a chapter or two of the current 'happy-ever-after' novel had helped. It at least took her mind off herself for a while. The experts, the family, and friends, the people who understood because they had been there, had told her to be patient, accept what was happening, give it time, it will come right. She wished she could define what 'it' was; she would like to bat it into hell. The tired but wired syndrome had been part of her life for far too long.

She took her bowl of hot porridge out onto the verandah. She enjoyed the daily ritual of watching the lumps of brown sugar dissolve into caramel, flavoured the pool of cream at the top. Her comfort food. As a kid she had seen faces in the sugar lumps, imaginary friends that she had silent, secret conversations with.

She surveyed her world checking the state of the tide and seeing if there was any sign of humanity around. She noticed the white yacht anchored out in the middle of the cove. It must have come in after dark.

Her daily morning walk took her up the wooden staircase to the flat land at the top. She liked to stop and sit on the verandah of the old bach and look out to the cove entrance then sweep her gaze back over the moored boats, the baches, and the bush, to the place where the harbour split in two. These arms or estuaries empty out at low tide becoming pathways for oyster catchers, blue herons, humans and their dogs looking for something they need. The elevated world made her world bigger and reminded her that she was not on her own. She sees boats coming and going, the scheduled shuttles and ferries as much a part of the Island's rhythm as the creeping in and sucking out of the tides.

She said hello to the pigeons that cooed softly to her from the tall kanuka trees that flanked the path. The faces in the trees seemed friendlier today. She hadn't always felt comfortable with them. She knew it was only her imagination that turned the shadows and patterns of the tea trees into tattooed faces with black eyes watching as she went by. They weren't scary enough to stop her walking each day. She enjoyed the exercise and also that the track took her to the other side of the peninsula and down to the sunny, pebbly, beach. Here she had a view over to the mainland with its beaches, houses and road to the city. She had driven up the road seeking the solitude, the distance, anything that would take away the pain of her life. She had been told that this was the place to come to heal. She was starting to believe it.

On her way back she started thinking about dinner, should she put the net out? Perhaps if she fossicked around in the old garden she might find some edibles. She was lucky, some late season tomatoes bursting with flavour, a handful of figs hidden from the white-eyes by enveloping leaves, and some perennial spinach. That's a good start, she thought, I still have some of that great cheese I bought from Puhoi – that's a meal, with or without fish.

The old men with sorrowful eyes looked out with interest as she walked the length of the jetty with her coffee. What was it with her seeing faces in everything? These faces were interesting though, permanently cast in the timber of the decking, each one unique. Perhaps I could immortalise them in woodcuts she thought, then became excited as the idea took hold and she visualised the resulting prints. Enthused, she walked quickly up the stairs to draw up the designs before the thought was lost. She was so engrossed she failed to see the guy in the dinghy row closer to the jetty than was necessary and watch her disappear into the house.

She couldn't believe that she had worked three hours non-stop in the studio. Three hours of total concentration. How good was that? She was lucky to have this workroom. She couldn't remember the last time she had been that excited and engrossed in her art. She was pleased with her efforts. Tomorrow she would carve the blocks and print them up.

Hide tide in an hour, time to get the net out and try to catch something for dinner. She'd been lucky most times, it had been worth the trouble to get the bin out of the fish locker and set it. She secured the longer rope to the bollard on the sea wall and walked backwards with the bin, allowing the net to pay out slowly, keeping the leads and floats apart.

"Can I help?"

She turned to see a man watching her from the jetty edge. A man with a face she had never seen before but one that was instantly recognisable and utterly familiar.

"Sure" she said, and they proceeded to pay out the net, working together easily until it was fed out and secured.

"I came by earlier when I saw you down here," he said. "But by the time I'd rowed in, you had disappeared."

She showed him the old men faces on the jetty planks and told him how they had inspired her to design some woodcuts. He smiled at her enthusiasm, and said he'd be back later to see what was in the net.

"It should be about five thirty," she called as he rowed away.

"O.K. See you then."

What the hell was that about she thought? No, don't think about it, don't analyse it, don't spoil the moment she told herself. Just enjoy the feeling of ease and naturalness.

He tied the dinghy to the cleat and came up the steps putting a canvas bag down on the bench. He went to the jetty pile and slipped off the loop. Together they pulled against each other to keep the net taut, keeping the leads down until they could haul it up onto the seawall. They looked at each other and laughed as they counted the catch.

"I hope you're going to help me eat some of these tonight?" She looked hopefully at him.

"Just as well I brought the wine then," he nodded smiling towards the bag.

As they scaled and filleted the catch she glanced at the old jetty men and was not surprised to see them smiling and winking. In fact she thought she heard a chuckle or two but it might have been the sounds of the outgoing tide.

Six Degrees of Separation

Lois E. Hunter

Kawau Island
2nd March 1934

To Whom It May Concern,

My name is Rose Sowerby and I have left everything as I have found it except for the removal of 30 guineas to pay for my husband's funeral and the costs of travelling to Christchurch to live with my sister. I put the original box into this tin deed box and wrapped it in oilskin to protect the contents from any further water damage.

I have never disclosed my find to anyone else. May you love this house as much as we did. I hope the enclosed notes will help you to understand why I returned Edward's secret to its hiding place.

Yours faithfully
Rose Sowerby

***

4th June 1923

I realise my husband and I would have been rich beyond imagination if I had revealed my discovery of this box but after our previous life I could not risk losing the life and love we have found from living on Kawau Island. Instead, keeping this treasure secret, I am enclosing an account of what I have learnt about the previous owner of this house, for the interest of any person who may discover it at some future time.

But first you may be interested to know how John and I came to live on the Island.

We bought this house, with its contents, along with the land lease from Andrew Farmer of Mansion House Bay in November 1920. It had previously been built and owned by Eddy Ching. It had been vacant for the past 10 years so there were a lot of repairs to do. We have extended the existing kitchen and added a sunroom.

We came from Mt Eden where John was employed as the prison manager, a career he hated but he was obsessed with the attached status and with living the high lifestyle his income gave us. Despite the advantages though he became depressed and was drinking more and more heavily. When John attempted suicide he was 'retired'.

We had only been renting in Mt Eden and because of our lifestyle we had few savings. Enough however to start a new life here on Kawau Island. It was the best decision we have ever made. John has finally recovered and now thrives on this outdoor life. We don't have much money but we manage: John by trapping wallabies and opossums for their skins and I am now employed by the Reeves, the new owners of Mansion House, who appreciate my shorthand and office skills. We have a large vegetable garden, hens, and a milch goat and there are plenty of fish in the bay. It is like an everlasting honeymoon which I do not wish to jeopardise by disclosing this treasure.

Rose Sowerby

* * *

NOTES ON EDDY CHING

I have spent some time talking with Joan Wallace, who lives over in Starboard Arm. When she was a young girl she worked in the Mansion House kitchens in the times of Mrs Eliza Thomson. Joan said she had a brief romance with Eddy but he was very melancholy and too much of a miser for her. One night, Eddy 'in his cups' told her that he never knew his mother or father. The only thing he knew about his family was that he got a birthday card each year from lawyers in Porthallow, Cornwall. It was them who also paid for his foster care and later his boarding school in Christchurch.

On one of his plant buying trips for his previous employer, Sir George Grey, Eddy had gone to Cornwall to find out more from the lawyers but had come to a dead end. All the lawyers would tell him was that his mother's family had paid for his upbringing and had insisted on their privacy. Eddy had left a letter with the lawyers addressed to his mother including his New Zealand address in the hope she would contact him. But she never did as far as Joan knew. According to Joan, Eddy was born in Christchurch on 25th February 1839, and died on 5th November 1910 at the age of 71.

Bill Johnston from Stockyard Bay told me that his father Jim, and Eddy were friends. Eddy would visit their home and the two men would reminisce about the days of Grey and as the level of the whiskey bottle lowered their singing increased. His father on the accordion and Eddy on the ukulele, or the Jew's-Harp he always carried in his jacket pocket. Bill called Eddy a 'shadow man,' as you could not see who he really was. He seemed to be there one moment and gone the next. Bill was yet another Islander who mentioned how Eddy was seen at strange hours foraging around the abandoned Copper Mines. Eddy's answer was that he was looking for the insects that he did detailed ink drawings of. The large painting of the rooster hanging on Bill's wall was painted by Eddy. Eddy had painted it for Bill's mother. It was of her prized Rhode Island Red. He has written on the back of it, 'It is not possible for the man I've become to judge the young man who first came to this Island'. Bill did not know what he meant by that.

Joan Wallace, knowing how I was trying to find out more about Eddy, invited me to her husband's 90th birthday party, saying there would be a lot of old timers arriving and some of them would have known Eddy. I was thankful I knew shorthand as many were eager to recall Eddy and with their stories cutting in on each other I could not always follow who was saying what, but hopefully the following is a true account of what I was told that day. I have put them into some sort of order.

Eddy? He was working as the head gardener for Sir George Grey. Became his right-hand man. Think he even went overseas searching out plants. After Grey left he stayed on and did the gardens for Mrs Thomson but he could turn his hand to all sorts of things. Skippered Farmer's steamer for a while. Did anyone tell you about his donkey? Can't remember its name now. He used it as a pack animal as he got older when his ankles started playing up.

Eddy? He had a good knowledge of mining. Said he learnt it from his years in America. An expert with gelignite. Came in handy to get rid of tree stumps. Eddy worked with Holgate and then Skeates when they were trying to re-open the copper mines. I heard somebody say they had heard that Eddy said the mines were what brought him to the Island in '64.

Eddy? Yes, he knew all about gunpowder. One New Year's Eve he put on a display of fireworks. Said he learnt how to from the Chinese when in the goldfields of America. Think that New Year's Eve was when Elizabeth was here. Not long after that she went back to England. He got tired of waiting for her to return and went over to get her. Didn't bring her back though.

Elizabeth? She was young, and tall for a woman, but Eddy was tall himself. Elizabeth had pale blond hair and a very sparkly nature. She came as a companion to an English woman who was visiting Grey for the summer. Eddy was smitten. They say that loners fall the hardest. Poor b***gar for everyone could see she was too lively for him. Surprised everyone that they had an 'understanding' but then she had to return to England. I don't know why. He was to build them a house and when finished send over the money to bring her out and they would marry. Leased an acre off the Mansion House Estate over in Bon Accord. He took three years to build that house. It was a real work of art, but she didn't return. He became more and more withdrawn. Become quite a hermit by the time Sir George left.

Eddy? What did he look like? Actually the first thing you were aware of was his accent. Got it from his younger years in America when he was working in various goldmines. It was over there he got the name of Eddy. He loved everything American. Named his launch *River Queen* after one of the Mississippi paddle steamers. Tall, he was tall, rangy, I think you would call it, but elegant; not sissy though. Carried himself very straight, right up until the day he died, despite the troubles with his feet. Always deeply tanned with the longest fingers you would see on a man. Artist's hands. Despite that he was a practical man. He would work at anything that was offered for the sake of another shilling. Eddy was always doing something, not one to sit around chatting. Don't think anyone was surprised when some of Eddy's paintings were exhibited and sold in London.

Saw some of his bird paintings, those birds looked as they were just about to ruffle their feathers and burst into song.

Eddy? He was a bit of an eccentric, but then islands seem to attract them, don't you think? How did Eddy die? We blamed it on that donkey of his. Fred he called it. He got the donkey to carry his gear around the place when his feet started packing up. You'd see that donkey standing on the foredeck of the *River Queen*, like a dog on guard, whenever Eddy was off around the Island. He often did jobs here and there around the place. You'd even see them going off to the Mainland to get in supplies. Fred had a definite personality, and stubborn? When Eddy got totally frustrated with it he'd say, "That donkey will be the death of me one day!" Seems he was right about that. Winter of 1910 Eddy died from the pneumonia he got after rescuing Fred out of the mud on an incoming tide in South Cove. Seems Eddie had gone out in his launch fishing and left Fred behind. Fred had escaped from his paddock and had come looking for him. Old Jim Johnston took the donkey over to his place but it died soon after. Jim reckoned it was from a broken heart.

* * *

              Kawau Island
              25th March 1989

Dearest Daughter,

If you are reading this then it means you have now got the letter I left with the lawyer for you. I never did get around to personally telling you about this fortune. I can only apologise most sincerely and deeply for not doing so.

Who would have known the old stone steps to the lower garden hid such a secret under them? They would have been the front door steps to the original house that burnt down in 1936. I found this tin deed box when I decided to re-use the stone elsewhere.

By now you will have probably have read Rose's letter and her notes, and found the bundles of banknotes along with the gold bars and the guineas Go quietly dear, even your closest and dearest can change their character when they smell the scent of gold.

I made some investigations to see if any of the gold could have been found on the Island. The Department of Conservation says the soil structures of the Island, though it has had a minable quantity of copper, could not also contain gold (see attached D.O.C. report) though many copper mines in U.S.A. have both copper and gold in the same mine. Eddy was known as both a miner and a miser, a hard worker always after an extra shilling, as well as a successful artist and portrait painter. There are a few undamaged banknotes, some dating back to the late 1850's from both American and London banks. It was not until 1914 that banks ceased to pay out in gold on the return of their notes. I presume the stamped gold bars and the remaining guineas came from them. The mystery is where the hand formed bars came from. When I visited you in Wellington, before you shifted back to Auckland, I went into that manufacturing jeweler in Willis Street with an unmarked bar weighing 450 grams, but the man got so excited at its purity and colour wanting to know how I got it and where it had come from that I mumbled something about being left it by my grandfather and its sentimental value and fled, turning down the $20,000 he was offering to pay on the spot, in cash.

Like Rose, I also struggle with the dilemma of what to do when I consider the consequences of sudden wealth. Not just the explaining of how I got it and probably attracting a raft of contesting lawyers etc. but the fact I really love this life I have finally found by living here in my little cottage. I watch the three of you girls having your struggles and yet gaining so much pride in each achievement you attain. Of course I wanted to share the fortune with you but at what cost to all our happiness? Better? Worse?

As executor of my will it is to be your choice now. The box with its contents is included under the general heading of moveable goods which includes household furniture etc. and their proceeds to be shared equally amongst the three of you.

I chose you initially to be my executor for your honesty and moral goodness. Secondly because you look so much like my maternal grandmother, Vera, whose Cornish grandfather was a Richard Ching. Serendipity?

In conclusion dear, it is your decision entirely if you wish to claim all or part of this treasure, or instead return it to its hiding place.

       Love you,
       Mother

Island Time

Lin Pardey

Marlene glanced at the shopping list she kept clipped to the dashboard of her car. This unexpected traffic back-up on the Harbour Bridge guaranteed she couldn't make all the stops she wanted and still catch the last ferry. "Okay, I'll forget the Plant Barn, just pick up some lettuce starters at the Mitre 10 along with the paint Colin needs. And we probably have enough wine to see us through till next week so scratch the stop at Farro's" she said out loud even though no one was there to hear her. She gave a chuckle. Each time she left the island she was sure she'd organized her lists and left plenty of time for her meeting with Elaine, the graphic artist she'd hired to man her mainland office. But, something always seemed to intrude, to take up any spare moments leaving her rushed, frustrated, talking out loud just as she was now.

It was almost dark when the ferry pulled alongside the jetty fronting their home but Colin was waiting, wheel barrow in hand. Even better, when they'd carted the bags of groceries and two boxes of builders supplies up to the house she found he'd put the casserole in the oven and started a fire. Colin gave Marlene a hug when she stated, "I hate the rushing every time I leave here, hate never quite getting everything we need, hate having to cut meetings short."

"Moving to the island was just as much your idea as mine," Colin reminded her. "You said the lack of interruptions would let you set your mind completely to whatever project you started and give you more time to play. But remember, we decided we'd keep the mainland house for two years, just in case this is all a mistake. Renter can be asked to leave any time. You just say the word. I sure got a lot done while you were gone. Come and see the new section of deck I framed up."

Marlene followed Colin out into the cold of late evening, stepping carefully along the planks he'd laid on the new framing. By going right to the edge, where an elegant hand rail would soon appear, she could see out the entrance of the bay. The lights of the mainland twinkled across five miles of moon-sparkled waters. The echo of a morepork's call blended in pleasant harmony with the slight whispers of the breeze-caressed trees. "Yes, this deck is really going to get a lot of use when it's finished, even in winter," she said to encourage Colin. It was obvious from the tightening of his arm around her waist that he'd been waiting for her approval. After only three months, Colin was completely in tune with island life. His strong yet light looking woodwork had already attracted job offers. He'd agreed to start work on an interesting building project just across the bay as soon as they bought a fizz boat big enough to use in heavy winds. He definitely couldn't cart tools across a kilometre of choppy water in the small dinghy they were currently using to get around . For unlike most places, this island had no roads, it was a true water based community – something both he and Marlene really liked.

"Come on inside, I'll help put things away after we eat," Colin said.

That was all it took. Marlene, tired from getting up at 6am to catch the earliest ferry, tired from driving through heavy traffic, tired from trying to fit too many 'should does' into too short a time, blurted out, "It's just too much." Tears began to trail down her cheek, "All the rushing, packing everything on and off the ferry, having to get stuff put away before some wild bird digs into my groceries, before frozen food thaws out, getting everything stored before I go to bed so I can get up and actually go to my office without feeling guilty. And as for my work, I had to rush out of the office just when Elaine was starting to come up with some good ideas. You know, I hired her four months ago and have never had any time to really get to know her."

Colin didn't say a word. Instead he took the building supplies out to his temporary shed. When he returned, Marlene had put most of the groceries away, the casserole and a tossed salad were set on the table. She acted as if her earlier outburst had never happened, chatting cheerfully, sharing interesting tidbits from her day.

The next morning, when Colin walked into the sun room that had become Marlene's office she was on the phone, the image on her computer monitor flitting from page to page as she talked, paused to scribble a note, then searched through more images. "No, I don't see exactly what you are getting at," he heard her say. "I'll try to spend more time with you next week when I come to town. Then we can look at this together. Definitely need some new thinking to make the Trelise fashion campaign stand out from rest. If we can get this one right, we've got a chance to get more of her work. Keep thinking on it Elaine."

"Sounds pretty important, why don't you go back to town and meet with Elaine tomorrow or the next day?" Colin suggested.

"Are you crazy? I don't want to turn right back into a commuter, wasting half my time on the road, wasting money on ferries. And I've got almost two days' work on the Johnson account; I promised to have it done before the weekend. I don't want to miss another Readers Group meeting, it only happens once a month and I missed the last one. Only way to get to know some of the other women on this island. Then it's Friday and you know what traffic is like. Weekend, I've been looking forward to our yacht club friends sailing in for a barbeque. Don't want to be too exhausted to enjoy that."

"Then invite her to come to the island tomorrow or Thursday night. You'll have the Johnson project done, so you can spend the evening with Elaine."

"Nope, she's got a four year old to take care of after kindy. I've got things planned. Next week will have to do."

"You and your tidy plans," Colin teased. "You hate anything messing with your plan. But Marlene, we both agreed we'd have to be flexible to live here."

Marlene pointedly ignored his teasing, but she did smile as she picked up the slice of apple cake he'd laid beside her morning coffee.

Two days later and midway through the afternoon, when Marlene happened to stroll out onto the almost completed section of decking, she was surprised to see Colin had cleared up all the scrap timber, his tools, and even raked the yard under the partially completed handrail. He was just wheeling back the empty wheelbarrow from the firewood storage shed. "You quitting early for some reason?" she called out to Colin.

"Yup," he replied then turned to pick up the last bits of scrap timber.

"Okay, what's up? You are definitely not acting normal. Someone coming to see your work?"

"Sort of," Colin replied. "I've made up the bed in the spare room, and organized dinner so this shouldn't be any hassle for you."

"You've what? Colin stop working right this minute and tell me what's happening."

"Won't be a surprise if I do."

"I hate surprises."

"You love surprises, packages in fancy wrapping paper - I don't remember to surprise you with presents often enough. But I know you love them, just can't stand being left in the dark. So suffer baby - it's only one more hour."

She literally stamped her foot and demanded, "Who is coming on the next shuttle? Why are they spending the night?"

But Colin had already disappeared into his work shop. Marlene headed to the guest room. It was almost exactly as she always set it up, fresh towels on the foot of the bed (she noted he'd put out two sets.) On the window seat sat an old basket she'd put out in the work shed with the intention of taking it to the Hospice Op shop. It was now full of cubes of wood. There must have been two or three dozens of the fist-sized blocks, obviously off cuts from the deck Colin was building. Okay, Marlene thought, it's a couple, they are interested in wood – maybe someone who wanted a cabin built? Since she'd just finished the Johnson job and didn't want to start on something else right away, she took a quick walk through the house. Relatively neat. Okay, she'd play along. She changed into a warmer (and nicer looking) jumper, ran a comb through her hair, decided to read a chapter of the book that lay on her night stand, but couldn't sit still. A bunch of flowers, must be something blooming on the hill overlooking the entrance to the bay. She could see the ferry coming in from there, be back at the house before it landed and play along with whatever Colin was up to.

Marlene was trying to appear nonchalant as she arranged the ferns and lilies in a big water jug at the kitchen sink (which incidentally looked out on the path to the jetty.) She heard young sounding laughter, then a lanky youngster came running up the steps, blond hair streaming behind her, a miniature rolling suitcase bumping and jumping along the stones of the pathway. "I saw three dolphins, a ray, a shag," she yelled over her shoulder. "Don't forget the mullet!" Marlene heard Colin yell through the bushes that hid her view of the path. "And a mullet. And soon we'll see a weka!" those were the last words Marlene heard before her employee, Elaine came into view.

Marlene would have been furious, would have lashed out at Colin, except for Elaine's reaction. She stopped, then began laughing and clapping her hands. "It's even better than I expected – it's stunning. Marlene I love it. Thanks so much for inviting us over – Lexi is having so much fun already. She and Colin seem to have plans enough to fill a week. Let me put these things down so we can eat the fish and chips while they are still hot. Here – grab this champagne, get it on ice so it stays really cold."

"Okay, you did surprise me – and it was a really nice evening," Marlene whispered as they lay in bed late that evening. Gave me a chance to learn more about Elaine, and I got a kick out of seeing you playing with Lexi and those blocks you made her. But I plan to tell Elaine this was your idea, not mine. Tell me what is really in your scheming mind?"

"Simple, I plan to take Lexi over to the Mansion House reserve, show her the peacocks maybe a wallaby or two. You and Elaine can spend the morning working so you feel you are caught up with your work. Then she can take the mid-day shuttle when you leave to go to the Readers Group."

"You'll lose a whole morning, won't have the deck finished for Saturday," Marlene countered.

"I can work a few extra hours tomorrow – set up a work light if I have to. You can help me clean up on Saturday morning."

The next day Lexi was clutching a peacock feather when she and Colin came rushing into the cottage just before noon. "Sorry to be late – I'll help get Lexi's things down to the jetty – she's taking the blocks home with her," Colin blurted out.

"No need to rush, canceled the ferry pick up" Marlene said. "Elaine and Lexi are coming to the Readers Group, take the ferry home from there. We've got the new ad campaign all laid out – It's a good one. And lunch is waiting for you."

The sun was nearly down when Marlene arrived home. Even from a distance Colin could tell she looked tired or unusually thoughtful so he didn't call out to her but kept working at his lathe, turning the handrail ends he wanted to secure in place the next day. When he finished and walked up to the house he opened the door to find Marlene sitting on the window seat, staring out at the bay. He poured two glasses of wine and walked over to join her. Her thank you, when she accepted the wine, was perfunctory. He waited patiently, knowing she'd speak her mind when she was good and ready. "If you are expecting me to acknowledge you told me so, you've got it," Marlene finally said. "You were right, having Elaine come out here gave us time to really work together, get to know her. Seeing her reaction to this place reminded me of why I wanted to live here. Only problem is, she enjoyed it all so much, the Readers Group, working in such a quiet atmosphere, wants to make this business meeting a monthly thing, offered to pay for the fish and chips, the champagne and her own ferry fares next time. But I didn't have the heart to tell her it only worked because it was your idea, which meant you had to take care of Lexi for us."

"It was great watching you and Elaine working together. Never really saw you in action like that," Colin answered. "I think it's a great idea. If it lightens your load, makes you feel more creative, I'll take care of Lexi for a morning each month."

"You sure?" Marlene asked as she moved closer and leaned her head on Colin's shoulder.

The trees across the cove began to turn gold in the last rays of sunlight. Colin relaxed, his dream still intact. "Sure, besides learning more about taking care of a youngster might be good practice."

"Good practice for what?" Marlene whispered as she turned to receive the kiss she knew was headed her way.

Laura

Diane Gray

Chapter 1
Starting Over

Laura's eyes opened with a start. A peep at the windows let her know dawn was on its way. From her window she could see the skyline of Paris in all its glory. Another beautiful day on its way. Just half an hour more she thought, as she snuggled down under the covers and tried to remember what she had been dreaming.

Lately thoughts of home invaded her dreams. Was she homesick? Or was her intuition saying her time in Paris was up? After all she had been here for sixteen wonderful years. But life was so different now. It had been six months since her soul mate and treasured husband Mike had been tragically taken from her. Instinct led her to touch the pillow where he should have been.

I really can't let this consume me today, I have too much to do. The charity ball that Mike had always organised fell on her shoulders this year. It was in two weeks and still there was a mountain of work to do. Thoughts of home will keep for another few weeks. One step at a time, everyone was advising, the grief will pass. Not likely, she thought as she swung her legs out of bed. As she opened the window the cool air was lovely and already the sounds of the day penetrated her thoughts, horns tooting as the Parisians started their day.

Later, all calls finally done, Laura made herself a well-earned coffee. From her window seat in the lounge she could see down onto the Champs Elysees. The hustle and bustle of tourists usually calmed her, but not today as she reflected on the last six months. Life can throw some curve balls at you, thinking back to the night Mike was murdered, all for a watch and 20 euro, ironically by the very people he worked so hard to support. The two boys who murdered him were from another city. They had no way of knowing Mike was the force behind the charity that fed and clothed them on a regular basis.

Laura will never forget that night. They had spent a very rare leisurely morning together. Mike's job as head chef and owner of one of the most elite Michelin star restaurants in Paris kept him on his toes most days. They had arranged to meet at the restaurant at seven that evening. Mike had a few things to do at the shelter that day but would be back for evening service. As Laura had sat and chatted to the staff, she couldn't shake a feeling of unease. It was going on eight, and still no Mike, and no answer from his mobile. Customers were starting to arrive for their evening, something just didn't sit right.

Now the tears started flowing as Laura thought back to that moment when the gendarmes came into the restaurant. As soon as she saw them she knew something had happened, the rest was a haze. Laura can remember Amy bringing her home and staying with her until her mum and sister arrived from New Zealand. And the funeral, how she got through she will never know. And there was still the issue of the mystery woman in the red coat, with a young boy about twelve years old, standing well back from the family and friends who surrounded her.

Later Laura was never quite sure how to approach Amy to find out who the woman was. Thinking of Amy, Laura looked at the clock. Nearly midday! Oh my God, she thought, as she jumped up, she was meeting Amy at twelve-thirty for lunch. As she threw on some jeans and a t-shirt, Laura thought, if anyone can bring me back to the present, it's Amy, a true friend, sometimes a pain in the butt, very direct, and not one to suffer fools.

Chapter 2

Friends

As Laura reached the café she could see Amy through the window and a warm feeling spread through her as she waved to her friend. Amy stood and enveloped her in a big hug. She could tell just by looking at Laura's face that she was suffering today. Her slender frame was shrinking by the day. Time for a tough approach thought Amy, no more feeling sorry, time was up for her friend, time to get back on the horse, so to speak. After Amy had ordered the wine she asked Laura how the gala was progressing. Laura struggled to hold back the tears. "My heart and soul are just not in it this year. I can't shake a feeling that I just don't belong here anymore." Amy took hold of Laura's hand. "Let's get this gala done, and then decide. You really shouldn't make any rash decisions while you feel like this."

A waiter stepped up to the table to take their orders. Soup and chunky bread sounded perfect. As he poured the wine Amy noticed him take a sideways glance at her friend. Even on her worst days Laura was a beautiful girl, the only person who didn't know it was her. Never stuck for things to talk about the girls filled in a couple of hours in no time. Amy was reluctant to bring up the subject of the gala ball up again, but she knew if she didn't give her friend a gentle nudge Laura would end up frantic.

"What are you wearing to the ball?" I can't imagine you have too many gowns that fit you anymore. I'd love to go shopping anytime. We could make a day of it." Laura laughed. Here I am in the middle of a life crisis, and you suggest shopping! Actually I would love to. Anytime would suit me." Laura hugged her friend goodbye, and as Amy made a promise to call her in a few days they both went their separate ways.

Laura decided it was too early to go home, work could wait. She found herself down by the Rive Droit, and as she wandered along the path people were all about her, enjoying the beautiful day Paris had to offer. How could I ever leave this, Laura thought. It would have to be to someplace very special. What had started out as an unusual day has turned out really fine after all she thought, as she headed back to the apartment. In a few hours she would be able to call her mum, and hopefully get rid of the feeling that something is not right.

The apartment was hot and stuffy when Laura returned and as she opened the windows to let some air in she noticed she had messages blinking at her. She opened the doors leading onto the small rooftop garden shared by her and her elderly neighbours, Henri and Adele Bachand. Smiling, Laura noticed one of them had left a lovely bunch of flowers for her on the table, fresh out of the garden. Laura inhaled the scent. Nothing like it in the world she thought. Henri and Adele were always leaving a little something out for her, sometimes fresh pastries, good books they thought she would love, all just to let her know they were thinking of her. When Mike was alive many a time she would look out to find him talking to Henri about the world and all its problems.

It won't be long before autumn she thought. The months are flying by. A warm Christmas would be lovely, but then there is nothing like strolling through the streets of Paris, wrapped up warm, with the Christmas lights twinkling in the trees, and people shopping for gifts. Stop daydreaming, and get on Laura thought, as she pressed play on her message machine. Caterers wanting to confirm last minute details, all things I can deal with tomorrow, she decided when she reached the last message. A call to her mum in New Zealand was reassuring. Nothing amiss there.

The next week flew by. Nearly all the arrangements for the gala were finalised, just one last thing for Laura to do. Picking up the phone she called Amy for a shopping day. Amy had lived in Paris nearly all her life and knew the streets of Paris well. Some of the shops they went into Laura had no idea even existed. Finally after a few hectic hours Laura and Amy settled on a beautiful sleek gown, shoes, and clutch. "Time for wine and food," said Amy. "No argument out of me," Laura replied. "Sooner the better!"

Over their meal, Laura decided it was time to broach the subject of Mike's restaurant, having not been involved in its running when Mike was alive, and still waiting for the estate to be finalised. Laura had no idea how things were going in the meantime, and as Mike's sole heir it would eventually be hers. So she felt every right to know how things were going. Amy seemed a bit taken aback at Laura's questioning. Having never had any interest in the place, why now? Laura explained that soon it would be hers and there were decisions to be made.

Amy was very quiet for the rest of the afternoon and Laura's gut feeling was maybe she had overstepped the mark with Amy, after all she had worked for Mike and was running the place now as if he was still alive. Apart from a new chef whose reputation was to be envied, all seemed to be well. She made a mental note to call the solicitor over the next few days for nothing else but to hurry things along so she knew where she stood financially. Not that she had money worries at all. Having had a dozen best-selling novels over the last ten years, she was a wealthy woman in her own right. Before Mike was murdered Laura had been half-way through her latest book. The publishers had been very patient with her, and extended the deadline a further six months, but deep-down Laura knew that for her own self-worth she had to start writing again. It was where she was happiest.

Chapter 3

The Gala

Standing in the entrance of the apartment Laura looked at herself in the full mirror on the wall. Hard to believe this time last year Mike had been standing next to her, telling her how beautiful she looked; she could almost imagine him saying it to her now. The elevator arrived to take her down to the foyer where the limo would be picking her up. Hopefully the driver would have remembered to pick Amy up first. Laura's stomach was in knots just thinking about the night ahead. She had rehearsed her speech a hundred times, knew who to thank, and not miss anyone out. When the night was done, it would be a huge weight off her shoulders. On the way to the venue Laura and Amy toasted themselves with champagne. Little did Laura know her whole world was about to be turned upside down again, and nothing would be the same.

The event centre was beautiful. The organising company had really outdone themselves, Laura estimated there would be at least five hundred people here tonight. A tidy sum had already been raised for the homeless from the ticket sales, and by the time the auction was done there would be even more. Her speech was scheduled for the beginning of the night, and it was nearly time for her to speak. Just a nod from the master of ceremonies and she was ready.

When Laura stood in the middle of the stage, a hush went across the room.

"Ladies and gentlemen, I would like to thank you for your incredible support tonight. As you all know my late husband Mike started this charity for the homeless and I am sure he would be very proud to see you all here tonight. I especially want to thank all the people who worked nonstop to make tonight a success." Laura went through the different people who had supported and helped her over the past six months. Finally she came to the hardest part of her speech. "It is with great regret this will be my last gala. I'm sure whoever takes my place will be as devoted as Mike and I have been."

As applause broke out over the whole room, Laura thought it had all been worth it. Looking out over the crowd, her eyes were drawn to a woman standing close to the stage. It's her! The woman in the red coat. As Laura watched a young man came to join the woman. His smile was a smile that, oh my God, the smile belonged to Mike. Beside her, Amy followed Laura's gaze. Oh no, not tonight, she thought, as Laura unfroze and started to move off the stage toward the pair.

Forcing herself to breathe and keep calm, Laura knew that Amy was only two steps behind her. Perhaps there was some reasonable explanation. As she approached the woman, she extended her hand and introduced herself. The woman looked directly at Laura and introduced herself as Catherine, and her son Edward. Mike's middle name. Amy stepped in and asked Laura if she would care for a drink from the bar. Laura got the feeling that the two women had met before. "Amy, do you know who this is?"

Amy's reply was very terse. "Not now Laura. This is not the time not the place to have this conversation." Laura looked at both the women, "Am I right in thinking this is Mike's son?" "Please Laura," said Amy. "Let's get tonight over, and we will talk then." In shock, Laura looked at Amy. "You knew, and you never told me!" "It wasn't my story to tell. I'm sorry." Laura looked at Amy. "You are my closest friend, and you knew my husband had been unfaithful to me, and had a child with someone else, and you felt it wasn't your story to tell? Amy, whose friend were you?" Laura was having trouble breathing. She didn't think she could be here a minute longer. As she reached the door Amy fell in beside her. "Don't be angry with me Laura. I could never have found the right words to tell you about Catherine and Edward. I'm sorry."

Laura kept herself in check all the way home. When she reached the apartment, she fell to bits. Her marriage was a lie. What her and Mike had was all a dream. How could he have been unfaithful? Surely she should have recognised the signs. Laura threw her dress on the bed and turned the shower on. As she stood under the water, the tears flowed and she sat on the tiles and sobbed, sobbed for the illusion her life was. Did everyone know except her? So many unanswered questions, for tonight she would just be. Pulling on an old pair of track pants and a t-shirt she curled up on the window seat she so loved, but the view had no beauty for her tonight. She thought about Catherine, were her and Mike in love? Was it just a one night stand? And their son Edward, did Mike see him often? Did they think she would never find out? She knew all these questions would be answered sooner or later.

The phone had rung several times since she had arrived home, but Laura could not face talking to anyone tonight. Amy had finally left a message to say she had a letter for her from Mike, should Laura ever find out about Edward. Amy was leaving it for Laura in the lobby tonight. Listening to her message, Laura couldn't imagine what the letter might say. Do I need this on top of everything else? But it will contain some kind of explanation if nothing else. At this time of night no one would be around to see her face blotched and swollen from crying. She made her way to the lobby. The letter was in her mail box. Upstairs, Laura settled into a chair and tore open the envelope.

Laura, if you are reading this I must be gone. I'm so sorry for leaving you darling girl and make no mistake I do love you with all my heart. Catherine came into my life at a very difficult time, and she was just there for me in a way I needed at that time. You were at the top of the best-seller list then, and you were travelling a lot. No excuse I know. I was at a crossroads in my life, not knowing if I was going to start my own restaurant or carry on working for people I didn't like. I never told you about my problems at work. I was so unhappy, and with your success I felt in some ways a failure and Catherine, a waitress at work, was there for me. I am so sorry, as this must be heartbreaking to read but you need to know the truth, and I am the one to tell it. As you can imagine, when Catherine told me she was pregnant, I was so torn between my love for you, and my child she was carrying. Catherine understood that I would never leave you, and in all fairness she never made any demands on me. By this time the brief affair we had was over, and the decision was I would support her in any way I could...

Laura's tears fell on the page as she read the letter. Had she really been so self-absorbed she didn't notice how unhappy Mike was? It was a long time ago. In her current frame of mind she couldn't really think straight...

Catherine and I decided she would have the baby and I would support her financially and help with any day to day problems. This may seem cold and calculating to you Laura but I could just not stand the thought of losing you and as time passed on I settled into a routine and managed to balance the two lives. Amy had joined me at the restaurant and became a great friend. Please don't blame her for not telling you about Edward. I needed a confidante and she was true to her word and for that I thank her. I am so sorry for causing you all this pain Laura and please know my love for you and being with you was never in question. I have no idea at all how this will affect your future plans. I just hope you can forgive me in time. I love you so much. Mike.

As Laura crawled under the covers her mind was full of Mike's letter. Part of her felt so sorry he had to lead a double life, and part of her was so angry he used her career as an excuse to have an affair. She and Edward were both victims of this. Hopefully tomorrow would bring some calm over the situation she was in. It wasn't Mike's face she saw as she drifted off to sleep, it was a young man's face that looked so much like his father.

Chapter 4

Decisions

Laura called down to the doorman and told him she was not home for the next week. She just couldn't face anyone at this time. For the next three days she neither answered the phone nor got out of bed. Her hair and skin felt disgusting and she simply didn't care. On the fourth morning reality hit her. Time to get up, stop licking her wounds, and deal with things. After a very long shower, hair washed and clean clothes on, Laura felt much better. A good hearty breakfast was the next thing on her list.

As she ate, she listened to all her messages, mostly from Amy worried sick about her, and a very timely call from Mike's solicitors to say they had the final papers to sign. The apartment was in Laura's name as she had purchased it when her third novel hit the best-sellers list. She had an idea in the back of her mind how to deal with Mike's estate. Certain she would sell the restaurant and go from there, she called and made an appointment for later that day.

With that done she called her mum and filled her in on the events of the last few days. Her mum, always a logical, level-headed person, was just what she needed right now. During the conversation Laura told her she would be coming home for Christmas, only a few months away. Her mum had suggested during the call for Laura to seek help from someone completely neutral. Counselling was something that Laura couldn't even contemplate right now. Telling a stranger she had failed her husband when he needed her was something she had to come to terms with herself, before everything else.

Getting a few mundane housekeeping jobs done kept her busy for the next few hours, then it was time to go. Laura was anxious about what the next hour or so had in store, and then had to smile, as if anything could possibly be worse than the last week. As she was ushered into the solicitor's office she couldn't help noticing what a very handsome man he was, old enough to be her dad, but very handsome. He introduced himself as John and pulled out a chair for her. John looked at Laura in the eyes and told her how sorry he was at Mike's passing. He then went on to explain the reason for the hold-up in finalising Mike's estate. His parents and a brother had made noises about contesting the will.

This came as a real shock to Laura, as Mike had not seen his family in twenty or more years, some misunderstanding over an inheritance Mike had received from his grandfather. Laura had never pushed Mike for any more information than that, but she did know he had used the money to set up his restaurant. John went on to explain that now Mike had gone, they felt it was their right to have the money back, however the huge cost of contesting a will was money they just didn't have, hence the delay.

Mike's will was very simple and to the point. Everything had been left to Laura apart from a bequeath of one hundred thousand euros to an Edward Lourdes. John looked up at Laura. "I presume you know who this is?" Laura replied that she did and she understood the reason for Mike leaving him money. John went on to tell Laura that he had received a very fair offer for the restaurant should she be inclined to sell. When Laura asked who the offer was from, he replied he wasn't at liberty to say but in his opinion it was a very fair clean offer to take effect immediately and shouldn't be taken lightly as restaurants were not easy to sell.

A tear slid down Laura's face. This was something she had already considered, and decided to do, but in reality it was a different story. She told him she would let him know in a few days. As she got up to leave she asked John if he knew who Edward was? He said yes, and he was so terribly sorry at the time for the decision Mike had made by not telling her. Laura thanked him, told him she would be in touch within a few days, and left.

Unable to settle when she arrived home Laura decided to go for a stroll through the city. The streets of Paris were busy at this time of the day. Parisians leaving work on their way home to their loved ones or drinks with friends. From the extremely rich to the poorest of poor, there was a place for everyone. Laura found herself outside Mike's restaurant. She could see Amy inside setting up the tables for tonight's customers. Having come this far, she pushed the door open. Amy's face lit up in surprise and she rushed over to embrace her friend. "Oh Laura, I have been so frightened for you. I have been wanting to see you. I'm so sorry for not telling you about Mike. I knew what he was doing was so wrong, but I just couldn't betray him." "Oh Amy," Laura said "Mike's choices and his behaviour were all about him. I am still me and really I can't turn back the clock, but I have decided to move on and have made some decisions that will affect you in a way. I have decided to sell the restaurant and go back to New Zealand for Christmas, then go from there."

Amy was surprised Laura was going home, but understood her need to get away. She also told her that the offer for the restaurant was from her and her partner and hoped that Laura wasn't upset. No! Laura could not think of a better person to be living Mike's dream, and wished her well. They sat and had a glass of wine together. As the evening's customers started to arrive it was time for Laura to leave. Amy gave her a big hug. "Keep in touch Laura. You deserve to be happy and I hope you find what you are looking for."

Chapter 5

A New Start

The weeks flew by. One more trip to the solicitor. Mike's estate and the sale of the restaurant finalised at last. Laura had already decided to leave the money from the sale in trust for Edward for his future. She had also considered Mike's grandfather's money to his family, but decided to leave that to Edward with a covering letter to explain that this was from his great-grandfather to be used wisely. Independent and wealthy, Laura felt that this was the right thing to do, as he was just as much a victim as her.

When Laura booked her flights home she had decided with time on her side she would have a few days in Hong Kong sight-seeing and shopping. Finally the day arrived for her to leave, a final look around the apartment, and she was ready to go. In the taxi she reflected on the last year, some happy times, and some very dark ones. Time to mend myself, Laura thought, and who knows, maybe find a little love along the way.

Landing in New Zealand, Laura was sure now that she had done the right thing coming home. She was staying with her mum until she found her feet, the weather was lovely and warm, and as the days turned into weeks Christmas came and went. It was lovely being with her mum and her sister's family for the first time in many years. She was mending her soul and starting to feel back to normal.

From her mother's apartment Laura could see out to the islands dotted about the harbour. Exploring the islands had never been on the top of Laura's wish list, but she decided to go and see what was out there. Packing an overnight bag she had decided to go to Waiheke Island. All the travel brochures made it look really lovely. Booking into a motel close to the beach, was a priority, so days could be spent reading, lying on the beach and exploring the rest of the island. It was just what she needed, and really now it was all about getting her strength back to continue with her latest novel.

The little village on Waiheke was really quaint, lots of cafes and friendly people. Laura spent many hours having coffee and cake, and chatting with the locals. Strolling along the street she glanced into a real estate agency window at the beautiful homes for sale. A small ad caught her eye. The views from the cottage were just beautiful, but the house itself needed a lot of restoration. Taking a step into the agency she found herself with an appointment to meet the agent there in the afternoon. Laura headed back to the motel to get her car, and had no problem finding the address. It was quite far from the little township, but the awesome beauty of the ocean and farmland was worth the drive.

The agent showed her through the house with the usual sales patter of what she could and couldn't do. Laura was really taken with the property and could just picture herself writing and spending time on the small beach down the path from the house. Laura had never really done anything on impulse before, especially something this huge, but she just knew it was right, and told the agent to prepare the documents for sale. Returning home to her mum she couldn't quite believe what she had done. Excited and apprehensive at the same time she made plans for the house, met with an architect, and started the process of building her new life.

Six months later...

Laura opened her eyes with a start, a peep at the windows told her dawn was on its way. From the window she could see the beautiful blue ocean. Another champagne day in all its glory, another beautiful day on its way, seagulls circling over the beach looking for scraps, their calls like music to Laura. She reached to the empty space beside her. The pillow still had the indent of her visitor. She snuggled down and thought a few minutes more. In the past six months her life had become remarkable. She thought of Justin and smiled. Laura really had to pinch herself sometimes just to make sure she wasn't dreaming.

The house was finished and Laura had been writing up a storm, her novel finished and a new one already on the go. Justin was the local builder here on the island. Laura couldn't believe her luck the day he walked into her life, she would have never dreamed in a million years that she could ever feel this way again. Only time will tell where it would lead, and at the moment she was happy and secure in her life, the past twelve months just a memory now.

Laura threw back the covers and went to the window. Opening it she could see Justin down on the beach sanding the bottom of an old dinghy. Opening the window and leaning out she put her fingers in her mouth and gave him a wolf whistle. Laughing he looked up, smiled, and waved. Life is perfect thought Laura, a far cry from the Champs Elysees, but Island life sure was the better deal.

Life is Sweet

Helen Jeffery

Why do the nights always bring disaster? Time after time, people can go about their daily tasks but then night arrives and under the blanket of the dark skies, all hell breaks loose. The girl was nicely tucked up for the evening and then the whole apartment block shudders, the sirens go off and it's out of bed, pulling on some clothing, grabbing the emergency bag containing passports, water, first aid kit, snack bars and torches, which always sits right by the apartment door and then making your way down to the shelter underneath the apartment block. Once down in the shelter it is just a waiting game, the ground jolts sending shockwaves through the room. Looking around the room there are several family groups all huddled together talking softly, a couple of young children crying but most of the people just sit quietly, pale-faced and looking shell shocked. This reoccurring nightmare still haunts the girl's sleep years later and any loud sound or bang still makes her heart skip a beat.

Her journey was nearly completed. Since arriving in this amazing country, torn away from her beloved homeland by circumstances beyond her control, she had revelled in the day to day happenings, some sad – like missing her family and friends back home, some full of fun – like the freedom to walk anywhere she wanted to and visit the market without fear, and some hard times like learning and understanding a second language and getting to know new people.

Her day always started with a walk down to the beach. She enjoyed the expanse of the wet sand and the patterns the waters made, like an artist free drawing on a huge scale. Some days it was very calm with just a gentle lapping on the water's edge and squawk of the sea gulls nearby. Other days the sea was angry, dark and noisy. On her return from her walk she would have breakfast and then would wander down to the village to buy bread and vegetables. This habit was a difficult one to stop. Back in her homeland there were no supermarkets, and all the shopping was done on a day-to-day basis, buying fresh food for the meals of the day. Here at least she always found what she wanted, back in her homeland she sometimes had to queue for hours just for a loaf of bread.

 She felt very lucky that she had found this delightful village market with its small central area containing a butcher, bread shop and general store. It was only a 15 minute walk from her home and after a few weeks she had stopped looking over her shoulder. It was safe here. The shop-keepers were very friendly and patient with her lack of English words. Her command of the English language was pretty good but she often got lost when people spoke too fast and a couple of months back she had seen a notice on the noticeboard outside the general store – "English Second Language" so she had enrolled and now felt her English was much improved.

 For many years the prospect of living on an island had always been a dream. When the war escalated in her homeland and it was no longer safe to venture out, let alone enjoy the normality of a family life and work, she made the decision to leave. Once this decision was made she started to explore the possibilities of emigrating to another country and found that her skills were required in New Zealand. A couple of years previously she had worked with a volunteer group within her own country and had maintained contact with one of her co-workers through email. She emailed her friend and a couple of days received a reply – he would be more than happy to help with her immigration process and also he knew of a company who may be happy to sponsor her.

 The waiting to hear back from immigration and the sponsor company was excruciatingly slow with many emails and letters back and forward and several Skype interviews, but finally 20 months after the first application, she received notice that she had dreamt about – yes she was accepted for immigration to New Zealand and the sponsor company were happy to take her on for a contract of two years but with one catch – they wanted her to work with a small group of medical experts on an island up in the Pacific group of islands, called Rarotonga.

The day of her departure from her homeland had been fraught with anxiety and apprehension but deep in her heart she knew this was the beginning of a new life and it was very exciting. Her arrival in New Zealand was very welcoming but extremely busy with a week's induction course by the company who she would be working for, and then a week later the flight up to Rarotonga and meeting with her work colleagues up there. The job was interesting. She worked shift work commencing in the afternoon through to midnight. These hours actually suited her; she was able to get enough sleep in the mornings and still had plenty of time to explore, or do her shopping before commencing work in the afternoon. Her life had become very routine - but living in this wonderful environment, with its warm days and evenings, the beautiful smells of the frangipani and ginger flowers and the friendly people - was a dream come true.

Late one evening, as she sat on the bench swing watching the moon slowly rise above the palm trees, she reflected on the past five years since the upheaval of leaving her homeland and the journey to a new country. She likened the moon's rising to her life, bright and beautiful in all its glory and the feeling of wonderment it bought to her heart. It bathed the bay with twinkles as the light caught the waves chuckling onto the beach. Her job here was rewarding, her work colleagues had opened their hearts to her and welcomed her into their lives. She enjoyed a good social life despite her restricted hours of work and she had found love.

Totally unexpected, Rupee had walked into her life, or rather limped. He had come to the clinic with a badly ruptured Achilles tendon so had been admitted into the local hospital and ended up staying for over two weeks. They had started talking during her evening shift and discovered they had many things in common. He had immigrated from India five years previously on the promise of a better life - a hard working life but still a better life and he now owned some land and was growing crops for the market. Their courtship lasted just over 10 months and when Rupee proposed, she accepted immediately. Because they had no close family in Rarotonga, their wedding was very quiet and informal with a memorable honeymoon on a nearby island and now they were expecting their first child in six months' time.

Just last week she had learnt that her brother's immigration papers had come through and he would be moving to live in New Zealand very soon. It would be great to have family nearby and not on the other side of the world. Sadly during the past five years both her parents had passed away, and her remaining sister had met an American guy in the forces and was now living in the USA. For the time being, her life was here in Rarotonga. She planned to keep working until the baby was born and then after six months go back to work. With Rupee being self-employed, they would be able to work out baby caring arrangements between her shift work and his work obligations.

Life on Rarotonga really suited her. She could travel around the island very easily, either walking, or travelling by car or motor scooter and even the local bus service was reliable. The main road around the island was only 32kms. She lived in Avarua, the capital of Rarotonga and there were many resorts geared up for tourists, all around the island. She found the island a very spiritual place, with many churches, and most families lived a Christian lifestyle. With the day to day tasks of working at the clinic, preparing for the birth of her baby and making her home a delightful place to live, life was sweet.

The Culling

David Kendall

There is green. There is viridian, verdant, emerald. And there is olive. He is of the olive hue, a man who strives to enhance greenness by killing creatures. An unsightly conflict, staining the path of the anti-hero.

Treading the parched brown slopes and exposed clay gullies under the island's manuka canopy, he is an earth doctor bringing dead land back to life. Smelling the decayed waft of the wallabies and possums he has poisoned or shot, he is a mortician.

He rubs his eyes, tired, gritty after another interrupted night. He did manage to drop off into drug-infused slumber. But the pain screeched back after midnight, teeth gnashing at his afflicted spine, the morphine relief exhausted. A pain as voracious as the puny snappers nibbling on the squid-baited no. 6 hook at the end of his line right now.

So more pills, more two-hour dozes.

In healthier times he'd be snoring by nine in the evening. He'd be awake before the sun, cradling the long gun and striding through Kawau's 5,000 acres of depleted woodland, baiting the traps, tallying carcasses—culler Brian, the hills formed his abattoir. It would be unnaturally quiet under the uniform spread of manuka forest with its sparse birds, its limited insect life, and its environment of scarcity.

He would pause at a lookout on Mount Taylor to survey the steep landscape.

It was not his domain—the only thing he owned was his past—more like his protectorate. There he might muse, imagining the cry of exultation uttered by a birthing mother when the new-born slips free. Such a joy, indiscernible to the human ear, must erupt from rooted nature when the last wallaby or possum expired.

Three months have passed since his gun has fired or blue pellets have vanished from his bait stations.

But today he's fishing. Tiny wavelets lap at the fat rubber dinghy and bounce off the rocky point just north of North Cove. Stone that gleams black and stark when the waves throw up spume, but grey today. The breeze says go south; the incoming tide dictates north.

Shorn of bark, sun-dried almost to silver, two manuka trunks with a shared root mass hang down the steep incline, marking this spot where fish congregate during high and low tides.

Touching his cheek—clean-shaven with a new razor blade—he smells the blend of soap and squid. He'd showered extravagantly after tidying up the rented bach, not turning off the water while he lathered. Winter was just over the horizon, and the tanks would fill.

A cormorant with a hook and trace trailing from its beak splashes down near the boat. He removes an undersized snapper off the hook and slips it over the opposite side of the boat. But the bird dives and seizes the released fish. It moves further off and swallows laboriously. After floating a few more minutes it lumbers off low over the water.

His line drifts and his finger senses the insistent juveniles ten metres under. But he's distracted.

The doc at the clinic last week was quite clear. Eight to ten weeks while the spine drips rot into the brain. Then: fish bait.

"I'd advise you to put your affairs in order soon as possible," the medic had told him, his delivery as unremitting as a scalpel.

He'd always leaned toward the environment. Humanity was an invasive species. So he and Linda had gone childless. And then, all too soon, Linda had gone. So there aren't any affairs to put in order. Not important ones, anyway.

It's a day since the clocks were put back. The sun is plunging through a golden sky, and he knows it's time to go home.

He stirs and his mouth hardens, the lower lip leaking, bitten sometime in the night. Hot embers sear his lower back, trickle lava through the left leg.

He reaches for the Styrofoam cooler in the bow just beyond his tackle box. A cold waft follows as he lifts the lid. The brown-tinted plastic bottle inside holds fifty-two pills. The printing on the label exhorts the user to employ caution in taking such medicine. It warns of dangerous consequences—to him, who is beyond danger.

The other bottle is, in fact, a thermos—a single slug of "Coruba" rum diluted in a litre of "Ceres" mango juice.

"Cheers," he says. "Sweet Linda."

Women are in the business of starting life, not ending it. Few are drawn to a culler, one whose livelihood is the snuffing out of lives. Linda is his life companion. Was.

He sips, gulps. Relief prescribed for a fortnight tumbles down his throat like fifty-two pebbles caught up in an orange flood.

He slips the rod handle between his bent knees, leans back into the stern of the boat beside the steering arm of the five-horse motor. The line from his spinning rig is tugging, wandering like his mind. A small snapper has swallowed the hook.

His eyes are closed. Linda is there, holding his hand, her silken skin glowing, coal hair pouring down her back. They're under the kauri tree, the island giant, the one the loggers of a hundred years ago somehow overlooked. His fingers feel her wedding ring, its elaborate Victorian silver holding an ancient drop of kauri gum.

"Forever," she whispers. "My Brian."

But forever has come and gone. Linda, six years of unblemished contentment, stolen away so early. She is there still, ashes nurturing the reprieved seedlings under the giant kauri.

"Together," he says aloud, then and now.

They fall asleep, there in the shade of the great tree. His head settles onto a pillow that is her breast and not just the side of his inflatable boat.

The line ceases its meandering. It moves slowly, then faster, steady as a train leaving the station. The drag grates, then whines. His knees close on his fishing pole, convulsive, unrelenting. The reel spins ever faster and the final loop of braid snaps off the naked spool.

    A second passes, two seconds. The water erupts 150 metres away and a mako shark as long as his dinghy catapults into the air. Again it leaps. A third time. And then once more it flings itself into the setting sun and it never comes down.

Beginning, Middle and End

Lois E. Hunter

No, no, don't go to sleep. Wake up! Help is coming. Talk to me. Talk to me. Start at the beginning.

Why does he keep shouting and shaking me? Start at the beginning he keeps shouting. Start at the beginning? Where is the beginning?

Swimming...I'm swimming...the sea is cold, I'm cold...keep calm, I must keep calm...find a light...head for a light...if in any trouble never swim against the current Dad said, go with the current and swim across it to get out of it...why am I sinking?...keep calm, think...my boots, get rid of my boots...take a big breath, duck under water... there's one off, now two off...breathe...jeans, they have to come off too...yes...I'm floating again. ...thank God for a calm sea....such a beautiful night... look at the stars...look at the stars...Aww, no, come on, don't go back to sleep. Keep talking to me. Come on. Talk.

Stars...stars...that's why I went out into the cockpit. To look at the stars...all of us in the cabin playing cards...wine...laughter...my friends, they are teasing me because I am off to have a lie down on the aft squab...but first I want to see the stars...my fingers reaching out toward the phosphorescence...I'm in the water... the boat keeps going away...I'm swimming...help...come back...I'm in the water...

Yes. Yes. Good girl, keep talking. You're doing great.

The waves rocking me...back and forth...back and forth...on stones... stones... I've reached a beach...I'm on a beach...I'm cold...cold...I must get up...walk...

there was a light...where's the light...doesn't matter just stand up and walk... anything, do anything to get warm...I'll die if I just keep lying here...there must be houses around somewhere...the moon is starting to set...hurry...I'm among the trees...it's dark, so dark...the trees keep grabbing at me...I keep falling ...what's that screaming?...it's...it's...it's there right behind me...ghosts!!...I'm running... running...now there's screaming in front of me!...run the other way...I can't hold back the terror...run...run away ...my feet...my foot...I can't run...the pain... wekas...I think I remember weka birds scream like that...slow down...breathe... breathe...lean on the trees...I can't find a path...it's so dark...I have to be in the middle of a nightmare...nightmare...I must wake up...I have to wake up...

You're ok. You're ok. The nightmare is over - you got here. God knows how. Shit girl you gave me a fright, coming home to find you collapsed on my doormat. Now girl don't freak out. Marty the medic thinks you'll have hyperthermia and I'm not to move you in case of internal injuries. Best thing to do was wrap us up together in blankets to warm you until he arrives. He'll be here any moment now. No, no, don't try to stand, lie just a bit longer. You've got a great chunk of wood stuck in your heel.

Hi Marty. We are over here. She's just opened her eyes. No I don't know who she is. Fell off a boat it seems.

***

Ah Carrie, it looks like that could be your boat pulling into the wharf now? It was great they agreed to pick you up on their way back from Great Barrier Island. And great you could stay the rest of the week on the island with me. I still can't get over how the skipper wouldn't believe it at first. When Marty contacted him to say one of his passengers was alive and safe on our Island he thought it was a crank call. No one had realised you weren't still on board.

Neil, I can't thank you enough for everything you have done for me. I have really enjoyed my time here with you and meeting your friends. You have all been so kind. It has been a magical holiday. Look, here come my workmates running up the wharf towards us so I'll say goodbye now before we are overwhelmed by them.

Carrie, my dear little castaway, let us say au revoir instead of goodbye. I think we both know by now that this is not the end of our story. We're just at the beginning.

Part two

Facts

How I came to Kawau

Ruth MacClement

My Dad grew up in Titirangi in the days when that meant gravel side-roads and full bush surround. Days when boys cycled to school in Avondale and got about bumping along 'metal' like a derby race on a donkey. Great Aunt May presided over the house-hold while first grandfather Richardson then, with her parents' deaths, Ouma kept the generous home kitchen garden in full productive order.

His was a 'broken family' in a time when 'single mother' was an insult to which even widowed and otherwise entirely respectable, even dull, women could not remain immune. Though Ouma was anything but.

So when through the natural course of events they made family friends and heard about Algies Bay, it was a greater freedom in summer holidays than I think we can fully appreciate these days with jets to Fiji cheap and baches growing beyond the reach of the average income.

Alison Roberts enjoyed a very attractive face, figure and voice and supported herself and her young family of three children as a singing teacher so was demonstrably accomplished but of course this was not all advantage in a divorcee.

The whole family moved to Algies Bay each summer...

Athol Algie ran a dairy farm turned sheep farm in Algies Bay though the soil was the same dense clay we all know from Kawau itself and the beautiful views saved nothing on the farm expenses.

The Bach was just that: built out of the salvaged windows and good-find wood of the day, painted with the most common paint or what was on special and of course used rain water and an outdoor loo. But it had a magnificent view of the whole of Kawau Bay, had the hill behind it to the south and a track down through the tall bush to the warm shallow water of Algies Bay beach. I grew up all my summers in that same Bach, sleeping under the table with my hand stitched quilt as the adults played cards or chatted until all grew quiet and I was long gone to the 'land of nod'. Sometimes I was lofted into an ancient bunk bed and smelled the familiar old fabric scent of rag-stuffed quilted mattress - the kind with the fabric-covered buttons small fingers would swivel and swivel 'til tight ...and eventually loose as the ageing cotton thread gave way. Always a burn across my back, always the temptation to dive into the frog pond - where the donkeys went to drink and where the water was forever the opaque ochre of clay glinting with electric blue or urgent red dragonflies. It was a place where jobs were done well and garden and building made with pride. The water-tank rotted before the bach did.

But when my father was a young man that is where my story of moving to Kawau really begins.

Having taught himself to sail entirely from books, David took little time to trial and master the wide array of techniques needed to navigate Kawau Bay in all its moods - and to read those moods with an eye to timing and waiting measured well. He would sail a small cadet sailing boat across the bay to Kawau Island and, here the legend is allowed to hold sway: would often stop in Stockyard Bay, a sheltered but easy to access anchorage to rest up for the homeward run. He would lie, I imagine, across the boards but out of the bilge and look up at the site where now we three live in a house grown from a place we've explored through day trips, annual clearings, three season tent living and eventually a roof that stands a gale force blow.

They were living in Canada with two small sons when the letter came, from Ouma that the west/central side of the bay was for sale: recently subdivided into a holiday resort of bare sections running from a solid concrete wharf and wall and newly named Poplar Bay. ...

As a child we all sailed up in a 25ft salthouse keeler, cleared an increasingly dense patch of bush for a Bach site and then sailed away each year... Wallabies bowed their quiet way through the undergrowth ... I don't remember Weka...but I do remember the birdsong.

Came out with Gavin to build a tent platform in the trees...

Moved out of our flat in Devonport and set off to the other side of the world: Bosa, Llanrhychwyn, Northern Ireland...

Came back to a south facing Grey's landing and the joys of a home right there on the water where our dream looked back at us from the sunny side point of the bay. Despite water running down the windows each morning drenching the fresh towels laid there the night before it was a sort of bliss...

Yes, we did love it - living on Kawau so that spring thru autumn we slept in a tent directly downstairs from where our bedroom now is...but the house was not to be built that summer so we moved to the sun of North Cove harbour mouth... Who ever said you can't have too much sun never walked about in underwear sweating in mid-winter. It was like floating in the crow's nest above a square rigged ocean voyager occasionally spotting the dolphins on their track across the way.

Walked over the hill. Grew fit.

Moved into an old army tent: khaki on the outside and glowing with autumnal orange in the mornings within. Over time that tent became headquarters, stored tools and muddy boots, collapsed in gales and was re-erected ...

Outside camp kitchen with shelves in the tree...

Grew too muddy over winter so the nightly move to a second, sleeping, tent where everything was laid out with Japanese delicacy made living a pleasure again. Movies in the tent from long power leads, the ultimate luxury.

Camp chairs we ate and lived from are still part of our furniture now...

Life now is here: with our little Badger, wekas and fruit trees - more than I dreamed but, when we forget to retrospect, less than hoped for. Life on Kawau really is the dream - the only thing missing is more time. Begrudge every moment spent from home.

The Mail Bag

Lyn Hume

The mail bag takes pride of place in our kitchen/dining room. These days it is no longer a yard long canvas bag, reputedly made by prisoners, with a leather thong to be passed through metal loops then secured by a large brass lock. Oh no – these days it is a small red satchel complete with a zip and a plastic locking device which breaks off when opening. The reason for the prominent display? A constant reminder of a dream realised.

As a young bride, nineteen years old and recently pregnant, I went with my husband for a ride on the famous "Cream Trip" in the Bay of Islands. It was a lovely, sedate outing with the old ferry boat calling at the various jetties on the islands. What caught my attention was the idyll of living on an island and receiving mail and groceries from a ferry delivery.

Several years later after having camped for several summers at remote Bland Bay in Northland we applied to the Maori Land Court to purchase a piece of land there. Accompanied by the Maori person with whom we had been in initial negotiations we turned up to an appointment in Auckland. Can you imagine our horror when we were advised by the Maori official for the court that the land was not at that stage for sale but as the iwi which owned the land was in many years' arrears for rates, pressure could be put upon them to sell their land to pay these arrears. After some very strong words from us that the court was supposed to protect their people from this sort of manipulation we left feeling disappointed but relieved that we had not been any part to such a travesty of justice.

A couple of weeks passed and I was wrapping up some kitchen rubbish in a 10 day old newspaper (as we did in those days) when my attention was caught by a two line advertisement under Land for Sale "8 acres, Vivian Bay, Kawau Island, own jetty - $21,000". Despite the fact that we did not at that stage own a boat, I decided to arrange for us to visit the property the next Sunday when my husband would be back from a trip overseas. We were duly picked up from the Sandspit, by the owner, on a glorious spring day and taken across to Kawau - our first ever visit to the island. Everything sparkled and shone and we were entranced from the moment we set foot on land.

After a luncheon of fish soup which was superb (the only fish soup I have ever found to be flavoursome) we went for a walk around the boundary of the offered property. Forty years ago the land was basically bare as it had been farmed for many years but small kanuka were starting to re-establish. The farmhouse at the beach edge which had been used as a guesthouse for many years had burnt down during the winter which meant that we would have to camp for several years but this was no hardship for us. Having decided that we would definitely like to purchase the property we were then told that the husband and wife owners would need to have a discussion as to whether we had the right auras to be the next owners. As our children played on the beach we spent an anxious hour hoping that we would pass muster. What a relief that we did.

For many years we put up tents on Labour Weekend and took them down again the following Easter. Nothing ever appeared to be stolen over that time and we really enjoyed the beauty of the lifestyle, visiting Kawau for weekends and during holidays. Eventually, however, our tents ripped and fell apart and a decision had to be made - new tents or build? We settled for what we in the family call our "ridged wall tents".

Finally, over 34 years after the "Cream Trip", I moved permanently onto the island and realised that I could organise a mail bag postal delivery and have groceries delivered by the local ferry company to the end of our jetty. Every grocery delivery, usually in a banana box and no matter that I know what I have ordered, seems to take on the feeling of unwrapping a gift.

As we are the first stop for the mail run I cannot count the number of times we have been photographed by tourists as we stand at the end of the jetty to hand over our mail bag and receive the next one. We always wave to those on board and wish them a happy time on the island and I can't help but wonder whether somebody else will have the dream that I had all those years ago and hope that they will manage to achieve that dream.

I Built This House With Others in Mind

Ruth MacClement

    I built this house for myself with others in mind. Each new touch, each careful choice of materials echoes with memories of good times in my youth sharing another's house and rebounds with dreams of sharing mine likewise.
    Building a house takes the sort of time and money investment that puts a soul in stasis. The goal of shared baths in candlelight, of home-grown meals about a trestle table, of sitting in the dusk with a whiskey, musicians and bird cries, of days of spadework rinsed clean with river or sea water and the flow of conversation ...all this gets immersed in the roller of work for money.
    Some days I completely forget that each hour of work is leading to a freedom from that workday existence. I forget to keep the friends and the contacts; I forget to exercise my mind and fiery spirit in readiness for my goal.
    That world is not forgotten, each friend is just as dear and beloved, and the self that wishes them near and feeling that joy I ever wish for them is only a day or two away from the last time I saw them.
    Meanwhile, Rip Van Winkle-wise, my workaday life does not fit them and that real world is now so far from the daily me in heels and a painted smile that the real me has experienced no time at all.
    To keep from crumbling - I'm made of fairly unblended substrate which depends on consistency to hold together - I infuse the work with ethics and genuine help but in some ways this makes the work seem more the real world

whilst the world of my youth that sings, that plays, that makes magic and new impassioned discoveries seems phantasmic. How can we so completely disconnect? How can so many have never in their lives lived that way? The real way...

So, I remember tonight ... listening to Mumby and Sons, hearing Tom Drinkwater, amid shattering ejaculations from G whining like a pragmatic chainsaw on a sunny afternoon, ... I remember that I built this house to share. To be that place I wish to recall where people come and open out.

This place will have trees, a welcome and good food. This is the place you come when you can't stand another human face, or when you want four hours of solid conversation, the place where you can stop in the middle of a meal or conversation and take a walk. This is the place where there is always plenty of good solid work to be done and the joy of release at the end of a day that only comes when that day's work is done. This is the place where all you need do to be welcome is to open your mind a little, tolerate variations in others, seek to live and let live (trying to leave things as you found them), and appreciate how good it is to be here.

There will always be room. There will always be little jobs you can do to feel useful, things that will show a result you can be proud of, whether it be for this night's dinner or 10 years of gardening. Someone somewhere has to be the repository of dreams - why not here?

Kawau – From Then to Now

Gael Archer

Chapter 1

The Beginning

Every human story is made up of a series of events - links in a chain leading forever onwards. Thus if just one step in my life were to have deviated left or right, I would probably still not be aware of the existence of Kawau Island.

The Archer love affair with Kawau was kicked off by a chance meeting with Lyn Hume in the North Shore Maternity Hospital, soon after the births of our sons Simon and Jarrod. For some years hence the Hume's and the Archers spent much of our summer holidays together at Matapouri Bay. Lyn's chance discovery of the minute "for sale" ad in a local rag sent us all off to view the piece of land on which the beautiful Hume holiday establishment now stands. It had been the burnt out site of the "St Clair Lodge". Little remained bar the old green shed - on the land now owned by Fay Richardson and Dave Lornie- and a very welcome operating flush toilet outhouse. There was no doubt in anyone's mind of its potential.

No time was wasted, the immediate focus now being on spending the approaching summer holidays in Vivian Bay. A 'tent' - ply walls and canvas roof on moveable block foundations - was erected to which electricity was connected, and which housed all food stuffs, cooking apparatus, etc. We made shelves out of whatever we could lay our hands on from the green shed, attaching them to the walls with string. Each family acquired the necessary tents and Foster and I carved steps up the hill behind the present Hume house to our family sleeping site. Tea tree saplings were removed to make the only flat land useable to erect our tent, and the tops were laid out on the ground to cushion our sleeping bags. I remember only too well the pungency of the freshly cut tea tree permeating the tent in the warmth of the evenings, setting off sneezing fits each night. It was a relief when our first camp stretchers became available, and we could get rid of those strong smelling tea tree leaves.

There was a bank to the forefront of the section in which Lyn and I dug our cooking pits – an Archer one and a Hume one, using improvised grates on which to set our pots and pans. Dinner devoured, dishes washed in bowls of water heated over the fires, children asleep and husbands back at work, we would sit back and gaze nightly at the inky sky dotted with myriads of stars, which we swore we could only see from this magical place. Then, kero lamps lit we would retreat to our respective tents to fortify ourselves for another day of children, sea and sand.

However, word very soon spread among the Hume friends and families that this was a very different and fun summer place to be. Thus the Archers had to move over and share our time and place with others. By now we were hooked, and realised, after three amazing years of communal camping with wonderful people, that we wanted more! We had become friendly with Raye Thompson who then owned the Paines' property on the point between Viv and Little Vivian Bays, plus two other sections to the north. One of these was going on the market, and we were asked whether we would be interested…silly question!! We scraped up the money and began our life up on the hill.

Chapter 2

Our Bit of Dirt

And now the work really began. Every inch of our new property was densely covered with tea-tree, and I remember watching with awe the speed with which the tuis navigated their way between the slender trunks, never missing a beat. But we had priorities. Somewhere to lay our heads, store our food and a toilet.

Out came the chainsaw and we were in business. The boys – Michael then around 12 years old, Andrew 11 and Simon 8, set to work helping clear the trees as they were cut and stacking them away from the planned sites for tents and our new shed. Each stump had to be grubbed out for tent floors, and for the next few days they each really earned their keep.

The big blue continental tent from down the hill became Foster's and my bedroom, and we bought an 8 x 4m army surplus tent for athe boys, friends and

family. It had ventilation flaps in the roof and windows with tie-down covers in the sides, and had to be waterproofed before being erected. That was a job and a half! Around each of these tents substantial trenches were dug, and carpet scrim was used for flooring. Our first beds were fold-up timber and hessian stretchers, and we bought two sets of collapsible wire and vinyl bunks, which when broken down gave us the extra beds we often needed. Lilos were on hand for the boys friends when they visited in the holidays.

Our first semi-permanent construction was a 2 x 3m car case purchased in Otahuhu in its collapsed state. It was ferried across to the Hume's wharf on the old *St Clair*, initially Lionel and Norma Barney's boat which was subsequently inherited by Piers Barney. The case walls were made of ply, but the floor was oil-saturated heavy timber, and when Foster and I tried to move it we realised we had a problem ahead of us. How to carry it up the hill on that narrow, winding track. We could scarcely lift it off the wharf!! This was well before the days of access from the Little Vivian Bay wharf, so the chain saw was put to further use, and eventually we somehow managed to manhandle each half up to our eyrie on the hill. I don't know how he did it, but Foster also carried eight concrete foundation blocks up that hill to put it on. Once it was erected, a window and a door were cut out of the walls. The window remained glassless but with the cut-out piece attached so that it could be used in the event of rain. The ply cut out for the doorway was reinforced to make a solid, lock-up door, pots and pans were hung on hooks on the outside of the front wall and Foster put up a rack for the lids, plus a kleen-sak attachment for our garbage.

The cable from the ugly old power pole which we were fortunate enough to inherit - ran through a hole alongside to power a fridge, electric frying pan and a jug. It also made easy access for bush rats to visit the 'pantry' each night, where they chewed their way through all of my Tupperware containers. I hated trapping them, as they were clean, beautiful, healthy animals, but it was us or them... I recall spotting one on a shelf one night - dark grey and white with a beautiful glossy coat, shiny eyes and most appealing to my eye. I told it to scarper, as I was setting a trap and didn't want it to be in it in the morning. Sadly that was the case, and I only too clearly remember carrying it out into the bush, tears streaming down my cheeks and berating its cold little body for being so stupid and not heeding my warning! I soon found a use for all those spare jars and old

tins my parents had stored away, and before long there was nothing left in plastic or cardboard in that 'pantry'.

The fridge was brought into the Hume's wharf, and we made a litter of – you guessed it – tea tree – and thus carried it between us up to the shed.

A long-drop was created with a view to die for. The walls were made from carpet scrim and it had no door (we couldn't obstruct the view!) and was also roofless. An old towel was hung over the wall to indicate occupation!

Try to imagine a rainy day and you *have* to go. Sitting there, too busy to enjoy the view, umbrella in one hand, toilet paper in the other attending to the business at hand, and trying to keep your trou out of the mud with the hand you wished you had! Our next toilet was a flash chemical affair, and this time we tied the scrim around four carefully chosen, evenly spaced tea trees, and added a roof of plastic mattress bags. Absolute luxury! Still no door...

Our first summer water supply came from the old concrete water tank which now belongs to Faye Richardson and Dave Lornie. Everyone who went down to the beach had to take two large dishwashing liquid bottles with them and bring them back full of water.

They were pretty heavy for small boys, and we tied the handles

together with rope so they could sling them across the backs of their necks. These were emptied into a 10 gallon plastic tank which stood on a beer crate at the hut door. An old Formica bench with stainless steel sink was erected on tea tree stakes, and dishes were done outside in all weathers.

In those days the Visor fireplace was in vogue, and it gave us the idea for the cook house. We had a similar shaped steel enclosure custom-made, with a spark arrestor-topped chimney and a decent sized opening in the front. Inside stood the grate under which we planned to light the fire. It looked perfect for the job, but most of the time the smoke didn't go up the chimney. After too many nights coughing and spluttering - on my knees stirring pots and stoking the fire - I resorted to wearing plastic goggles for eye protection, and occasionally when things were at their worst, a snorkel which sometimes helped improve the condition of the air I breathed – depending on which way the wind was blowing! My most memorable achievement was the successful completion of a corned beef dinner, with spuds, carrots, cabbage and sauce to accompany the meat. I arranged the fire to keep the meat simmering at one end, stoked another part up to bring spuds and carrots to the boil, then cooked the cabbage and stirred the sauce without getting either face or hands singed.

From somewhere we acquired a large sheet of ply which served as a table-top, supported at each end on more beer crates. We sat around this on collapsible camp stools to eat our meals. Food was laid out on an old drop-sided wooden table, in the middle of which a hole was drilled to accommodate the beach umbrella thus keeping the sun – or rain – off the food. We found that cable reels made very good tables, so we painted the big one we had and used it for draining the dishes in the sun. The campsite was lit at night by kero lanterns hanging from hooks screwed into trees. We were home and hosed!

Foster put a lot of thought into my Christmas present that year. Our army surplus tent made him think of the TV programme "Mash" of which we were keen followers. From the letters M-A-S-H he got "Mother Archer's Seaside Home" and so he had a sign made - to hang on the shed - to that effect (it now hangs on the front of our log cabin). When I first saw it I didn't know how I felt about being known as 'Mother Archer' – it sounded so old!! Then I recognised something he hadn't. The initials also stood for the names of our three sons, Michael, Andrew, Simon (from oldest down to youngest) and our dog at the time – Hamish. From then I was sold!

Year two saw a few home improvements that were sorely needed. So that those on dishes duty could function under cover, and to provide a greater roof area for water catchment when we finally got our exciting new storage tank, a lean-to was added to the side of the hut. This also enabled dinner prep and laundry to be done out of the sun or rain, which pleased me no end! The 1,000 gallon corrugated iron tank was brought over on the roof of the *St Clair*, and parked by the hedge at the end of the Hume's' wharf, waiting for manpower to get it up the hill. For some reason everyone who walked past it always gave it a whack, for it made a resonant boom which tickled the fancy of some. After a while the residents in the Hume camp became brassed off with this constant interruption to their peaceful existence. So, unbeknown to us, a contingency of blokes decided to get rid of our tank by heaving it up the hill past their tents and rolling it along the ridge in the general direction of the Archers'. Weren't we just too lucky?

After a visit to Dick Souness's log cabin at Pembles Bay, we began thinking along similar lines for our house, when we were ready to upgrade from our present idyllic set-up. We wanted to place it forward of its present position, perched over the top of our existing track. However, due to the wind factor, we were advised that it would be safer, and a lot easier to construct, if we placed it where our Mash tent was then sited. This was still a long way off, of course.

The following Christmas was a wet one. We had six children in camp, and a dear friend to give me moral and physical support. It rained and rained and rained. For the whole of January it rained. The children had 'tent' fever

and were becoming very crotchety, making life for Flo and I pretty difficult trying to keep them entertained in their confined space. One morning the trenches around my tent overflowed, and I stepped out of bed into running water! The day the sun finally showed its face Foster and Flo's husband, John, were due to join us. What met them when they reached the top of our track will never be forgotten. The clearing in front of our camp was littered with steaming tent gear. Damp pillows, sleeping bags, mattresses and clothing were draped over stools and anything else that was available to help dry them out. It was a sight for sore eyes – not. Then, when I discovered that all of my clothing that was hanging in the continental tent had developed a chronic case of mildew I decided – enough!! It is time we built that house!!!

Chapter 3

The Log Cabin

After much planning and consultation with the company "Bushhaven", from which we purchased the eight-foot modules for our house, we were under way. The bulk of the building materials were brought into the Bay by barge, and from there flown up to the site. A team of men on the barge and three on site were kept frantically busy loading and unloading at ultimate speed, in an attempt to cut down on expensive chopper time. There it all was – bricks, logs, decking timber, builders mix, cement, steel framing, rocks, concrete blocks, sand, gravel, particle board flooring – all laid out in neat piles ready to go. Our wonderful neighbour, Jock Redfern, was one of the on-site team, and his help – throughout the building process – was invaluable. He had a beautiful old kauri beam from an Onehunga warehouse which he offered us for our mantelpiece, as the pine one that we had ordered failed to arrive. It was set into the rock chimney by the fireplace craftsman, Dean Watson from Warkworth. This man was a perfectionist. The rocks for our chimney were hand selected from the Matakana bluestone quarry and choppered in with the first drop. As you would expect, there were a few casualties as they were released from their carrying case. Dean created his inside masterpiece first and then on to the outside. He completed the entire chimney with the exception of the small eastern face, but then ran out of rocks that were acceptable to him. As that aspect was impossible to view at close hand, we assured him we were happy for him to piece together the broken bits to finish the job. But not Dean. He went back to the quarry, hand-picked the rocks he needed, brought them back in his runabout and wheel-barrowed them up the hill from Little Viv.

The house was completed in stages, as money became available. It was a closed in shell by the following Easter (with the exception of the big hole for the chimney which had yet to be built) and we were determined to sleep in it immediately, hole or no hole. It was a freezing night, but we lined up the five little stretchers at the far end, loaded on extra blankets and snuggled in, savouring our first night's sleep in our new home.

Now that the roof was on we had the means to collect water, and we bought the then popular, rather attractive, wooden variety of water tank with a plastic lining. It did look good, and served us well for nearly twenty years, when the roof started to cave in, so we replaced it with the present green plastic job. The timber from the old tank has proved useful for the grandchildren's building creativity and for edging gardens – nothing ever wasted on this island!

We had a problem with the kitchen bench. It had been designed around two-inch tiles, but as we had just converted to the metric system the equivalent were slightly bigger, and I had to rethink the whole deal. I shared my problem with Jock and he told me what to buy, for I was faced with an awful lot of cutting. The task proved beyond me, having never realised how hard some ceramic tiles could be. Foster came to the rescue and found an outfit in town to do the job mechanically.

When it came to the inside layout, it was decided to have a large open plan living area with a bed-couch near the fire, plus one bedroom and a bunk-house for the boys. A walkway was extended from the front deck to their sleeping quarters. It wasn't long before the flimsy bunk set we initially bought was not up to carrying the weight of our growing lads, and we hired Jock to build us the sturdy affairs that we are still using today. After the ceiling and interior cabin walls of Douglas fir were in place, it was my job to stop all the nail holes before applying the polyurethane. The grain in this timber is multi-coloured, so Jock made me up pots of different coloured fillers, and I had to match them with the appropriate colours in the timber. What a neck-breaking job that ceiling was!!

As soon as the deck was complete we brought over an old wringer-style washing machine, which we set up outside the back door. The wringer only went one way and the thing leaked like a sieve. We filled it with the hose, and the water had to be kept running in during the duration of the wash. It was emptied straight out through the deck, and refilled with rinsing water once the wrung out clothes were replaced. A primitive affair by today's standards, but I was grateful for it then, as it sure beat washing the lot by hand!

As our boys each approached six-foot in height, we realised the bunkhouse was becoming barely adequate. To preserve our privacy we had bought the section on our western side, and so the idea of building a place on it for them was born.

Chapter 4

The Boys' Place

Our youngest son, Simon, who at the time was a practising architectural draughtsman, began putting together a design for a communal affair, using some simplified ideas from the Hume's grand set-up down the hill. A private unit for

each family and a communal living area, all joined by miles of decking, was built by Brett Archer – son of Ron Archer of North Cove – and his building partner. By this time we had legal access to the Little Vivian Bay wharf, and the concrete mixers, front-end loader for moving heavy stuff, plus a digger and all building materials were brought up the track which adjoins our boundary. It really turned into a family affair, with the boys and their friends, Foster and Simon's wife, Steph, pitching in at weekends.

Andrew bought an old tractor called

'Snoopy' for hauling purposes, but as this was pre-concrete road days and the ground was wet, Snoopy couldn't handle the slippery conditions. Kevin Wallace from North Cove lent us his four-wheel drive job and brought it round on his barge, the *Tardis*.

The foundation poles were massive, and each of the longest took eight guys and Steph to lift them from the barge to the landing above the wharf. From there they were picked up by chopper, flown up and placed directly into the appropriate pre-prepared holes. Therein lies a story.

One whole weekend was set aside for the drilling of the foundation holes, and it was a disaster from whoa to go. Nick the Maori (as he was affectionately known by son Andrew and our family) who was hired to drive the digger, had estimated that he would need every hour available to get the job done. The machine was loaded onto the barge at

Sandspit on the Saturday morning, and the barge broke down. Naughty words!!! The problem wasn't sorted until early that evening, so Nick, with the aid of many torch bearers, had to work through the night and Sunday so that we could return the machine for another job on Monday. Mission completed, he set off to drive down to the wharf late Sunday afternoon – when further disaster struck. One of the tracks came off the digger at the top of the road down to the wharf. In spite of Nick's expertise, and plenty of manpower, they couldn't get it back on. Finally, now late into the night, Nick phoned his boss in Auckland, who had to leave the warmth of his bed and drive up to Sandspit, come across in his runabout and sort things out. He was not a happy man. A night to be remembered!

Back to the holes. As you can imagine, not all of them were placed as accurately as required, and some had to have a few extra inches of clay dug out. This, of course, landed back in the holes, and it fell to the unfortunate builders' apprentice to remove it. We found a large, empty, 'Wattie's' peaches tin which we wired onto a long pole. The poor lad was upended into each hole, held by his feet while he scooped up the offending material, and hauled out to empty the tin.

The digger was also used for ditches needed for drains and cable laying. On one occasion, it was parked on our front lawn, side on to the slope, when Stevie, the operator, climbed aboard. He must have leaned out seaward for a moment, because to our horror, we watched the machine start tipping away from us. I've never seen so many people move so fast. It took the weight of seven bods to right it, averting yet another disaster and possibly saving Stevie's life. The gods were smiling on Stevie that day.

Eventually the project was completed. The units, though identically designed, soon had each son's individuality stamped on them, and a new era began for the Archer boys. However, one thing was missing. A holiday place needs a spa pool, so the boys got together and added a drop-down deck overlooking the Bay to accommodate their extra luxury.

Chapter 5

The Garden

Our awareness of Kawau's plight re the regeneration of its native bush, had been heightened during our relatively short period of time in residence, and we couldn't wait to start a planting program. My enduring love of NZ natives was born.

With each visit came trees, trees and more trees. Bags of compost, dolomite and fertiliser, plus gypsum to help break up the clay. There were wallabies galore on the property, so each tree was ring fenced and firmly staked to support it against the wind.

It didn't take long to realise that there was no future for me in this type of gardening. I now had the space to create my dream, and I knew that it didn't entail having to protect every plant we put in. In my perfect world fences didn't belong in the bush, but I eventually had to accept that it was the only way to move forward. And so Ian Rice and I began constructing the fence that, until recently, has protected our garden from the voracity of Kawau's wallaby population.

Our garden 'grew' in a haphazard sort of a way until Simon and Steph decided they would like to get married on the property. This made us take another look at things, and a new plan was hurriedly developed. Over the following six months the garden was everything. Structure was the goal, and it became our driving force. We gardened from morning to dusk, until it was time for me to set aside my trowel and gloves, accept what I had achieved, and concentrate on planning this wedding. Foster carried on. I was to cater for just over 100 guests from our little log cabin kitchen. It was quite a challenge, but our previous café ownership and my love of cooking made it seem a plausible venture, and I had many offers of help along the way.

We always knew we wouldn't be able to maintain a garden this size for ever, and that time has come. I create order and the wekas create chaos. With each easterly storm comes more work, we clean up the mess in time for the next one, then we start again. So, I am working on the acceptance that nature will take its course - as I always knew it would.

Toby

Jenny Gibbons

The day young Toby came to the Island, I think everyone thought I had lost the plot. I can still see Dave Jeffery's face on the Sandspit wharf, watching me and my new found friend board the Ferry. Heads were shaking.

Toby was only 6 months old and came straight from his mother, so I became his new mum. He was a little lost and looked to follow anyone, or any dog, that moved. He followed me down the wharf to get the mail, and all the tourists were out on the top deck of the ferry with cameras out.

Toby was very different from the big horses I had owned, very clever and very mischievious. One day while I was gardening he came up to me, with a white nose and white up to his knees. I sniffed but there was no smell. What had he been into? Perhaps he had been up in weka village, into Eric's plaster? What was this white stuff? Then our neighbours came down the wharf after being out fishing with their children, who Toby loved and hung out with. I told Rachael about this white stuff and she had no clue, until 10 minutes later when she came over: mystery solved! They had left a 5kg bag of flour on the kitchen floor. Toby had gone in, bitten the bag and poured the flour on the floor. Fortunately Rachael was laughing about it, but I was not very impressed with the little buggar, so I made him sacrifice his carrots, and used them to make a carrot cake with cream cheese icing.

Toby liked riding on the ferry. Captain Lawrence even invited him to walk through the ferry. When we got back to the Sandspit all the cameras came out again. And then he did poo. And Eddie was out with a plastic bag and scooped it up for his garden. I gathered his poo up every day. Our garden never looked better.

Because he needed so much company I sent him to my friend in Wainui where he hangs out with four other miniature horses.

I Love Brash Tuis in the Springtime

Ruth MacClement

I love brash tuis in the springtime.

This morning I woke to scratching, battering, thumping I…a rat in the ceiling? A possum on the roof? A sparrow caught in the chimney? Forget the sounds of bush huts of the past and winter. This fine spring morning a young bravado was battering our windowpanes, ferocious in his ardour - for what I can't quite tell - narcissus? He sized me up through the double-glazing as I washed & dried my face, "You looking at me? Huh?huh? You looking at me?" His tail flicking as he bounced on the railing, eyes levelled, he poised like a professional boxer preparing for a double-jab. The effect was only spoilt, a little, by the blossom stamen protruding from his bill. He chuffed and chortled his most impressive threats - only a little choked by drunken enthusiasm.

Minutes later, with my cup of tea, book and water view all bathed in bright eastern sun I hear the trill of morning chorus in a slightly different light: a dozen liquid calls meld in a serene medley of, "You looking at me? Huh?huh? You looking at me?"

The Dolphins Came Today

Ruth MacClement

The dolphins came today to visit our bay.

The bursts of breath, like athletic men panting through a snorkel, were the first clue. So close I could taste the salt, ozone and wet skin of him. Breaths came regular and often, catching it after exertion, and the youthful gangs of tui yobbos couldn't drown it out - so they moved to melodious competition punctuated by weka roll-calls

At first it was one enormous beast, grey in the water, a trail of surface disruption ...

All in the mind? Then, resolving into dolphin fin, it was enormous! A whale?

A pod of dolphins swimming in such close formation they seem to be one panting beast, blowing and gasping for air every few seconds.

Around and around they're going, for an hour? Just in our little bay, with the water near the high and the dolphins now so loud and expressive in their expelled air the seabirds take offense and launch a shrieking low flight over their heads, tuis battering the air as if to fluff pillows with their energy. It is the oyster catchers who are offended most and persist in the persecution 'till the deafening white noise of a water taxi arbitrates for a minute and the world resolves back to its scorching summer sun, rippled water and panted breaths of the swimmers circling round and around in the bay.

Lessons the Wekas Teach

Ruth MacClement

Quiet, cool and brushed with sunlight
the hills around my home are resting before the day.
Syncopated shrieks make jazzy rhythms of weka calls
rebounding and building across the valleys and,
as the sun reaches golden misty fingers through my windows at last,
the tui cut in with percussive exposition and syrupy rills.
Pied stilts on the foreshore weigh in
with merengue rhythms.

Morning has broken,
like the slow heat of a glass
before it shatters...and then grows still.

I sit now in a challenge confronted and overcome.
This is my house, my home,
my monument to a thousand tiny well considered choices and,
despite the array of things unintended, unwanted and unfinished,
it is complete.
Enough.
A grand folly of a home but mine and an achievement I too often disregard.

Wekas rebound the call till it must have traversed the island
and harks back to a more diffuse sound
- of grandmothers calling cooooo-ee! on a summer's afternoon
from the house on the hill to the beach far below
where grandchildren and oystercatchers wade in the silt and shallows.

This restlessness, dissatisfaction and even self-deprecating depression are what make me and each weka a high achiever. Also what make me unable to get out of bed some mornings and ready to break when life is fine - or in the case of a weka, dash kamikaze style out of the bushes as decoys in spring.

Play to these strengths:
nothing is ever good enough?
Then fix the things you can today
and leave tomorrow populated only by fantastic dreams and projects.
Each dawn, take stock.
Each night, dream a new dream.
Each day: do only that which can and will be done today.

A 40 Year Journey to Kawau

Cheryl Hoyle

When my sister-in-law Sue moved house last year she found an old photo of Steve and I that she had taken in January 1968. I was 19, Steve 21 and we had become engaged the previous December. Steve had graduated from his air force wings course and had been posted to Hobsonville air force base. I was living at home in Christchurch with my parents. At the end of December I had flown up to Auckland to have a holiday on Steve's parents' motor launch, *Acquiese*.

Up until then my boating experience had been limited to paddling down the Avon in a hired row boat and the inter-island ferry. The Avon was fun, usually water fights with friends and if you fell out it was not a problem, you could stand up and hop back in the boat. The interislander thanks to a few rough trips usually had me turning green by the time we reached the wharf at the other end and in no way eager to make another trip.

I can still remember the holiday. Everything was perfect. *Acquiese* was a 42ft long bridge deck launch and chugged along at 8 knots and 9 if you really pushed it. The weather was perfect for lying sunbathing on the decks, the fish were plentiful, the water like glass, it was a whole new world and I loved it! We chugged from Auckland to Kawau at a leisurely pace anchoring when we felt like it and arrived at Kawau Island in Mansion House Bay on New Year's Eve. There were so many other boats, laughter, music, bubbles and a clear starry sky. To me it was magic. I could have spent the rest of my life there. I said to Steve, "We've got to come back here some day and stay longer."

The holiday remained a happy memory for the next 39 years. During those years we had mainly been based in Christchurch with two brief stints in Singapore and England. Thanks to Air New Zealand travel we visited many beautiful places around the world but home was always better. When Steve retired in 2007 we spent a year in Auckland. By the end of the year we had decided not to return to Christchurch to live. We had no family left living there, two of our children now lived overseas and Will and his family were in Auckland. We wanted to live somewhere nearer to them but not on their doorstep and preferably where we could see water. I remembered Kawau Island and looked through the internet for houses for sale. I made appointments with real estate agents and told Steve we were off to Kawau Island for the day. It was October, the weather was sunny, the water like glass; it was as I remembered. Things may have turned out differently it there were a few white caps around but it was a week after we came to live here that I had a rough water taxi ride. We looked at several houses around the island and on our second visit we walked up the hill at South Cove. We went through the gate of "Tigh Na Mara" and looked at the view out to sea and fell in love with the island again!

That was it! Sold! We returned to Christchurch at the end of the year, packed up our life there and told our friends. The general reaction was one of disbelief and confidence that it wouldn't be too long before we were back. In June 2008 we moved here permanently, it had taken 40 years to realise the dream of 'staying a little longer' on Kawau Island.

It wasn't until last year when Sue sent us the photo that we realised we had anchored in South Cove in January 1968. The photo shows us on the beach here standing with our sizable fish. Of course there were no houses, road or wharf then but if you look carefully you can see the Coppermine behind us to the right edge of the photo. It was fantastic to think that those footprints we made then were the start of our journey up the hill. It just took us a while to get there!

Butterscotch Sun

Ruth MacClement

Butterscotch sun. Warm, rich, with a hint of intoxicating liquor.
It retells the scenes of childhood amid the rush, shush, plink and plonk
of a boat-filled coast. Warms the smile-wearied muscles of the face,
holds me close with the suncream scent of aunties' hugs and burnt-skin arms.
Now we're 'grown-up', we must keep the wrapper between us and the sun,
 abstain from butterscotch: prudence to guard against the transformation to
plump prune bodies.
Never fear, it is a NZ spring:
a gentle drizzle falls to save my skin.

I'll Never Want to Leave Soon

Fay Richardson

My first introduction to Kawau Island was when I met Dave Lornie, 23 years ago.

He soon brought me up to stay at his Aunty Janet MacIndoe's bach in Vivian Bay, to share with me the special holiday home where he had spent so many years with his parents, Colleen and Ian.

It didn't take me long to see why, away from the mainland, it was like being on your own treasure island.

Over the years I became more and more reluctant to leave when our annual March break was over. While we were unloading our rubbish at Sandspit and readying the boat for the long journey home, I used to look at the notice board for places for sale. That progressed to getting the real estate listings online.

Dave would look too, but it always ended with "If it's not Vivian Bay I'm not interested." Of course there had been nothing for sale in Vivian Bay for twenty years. We often lamented the fact that his parents had seen land for sale on Kawau in earlier years but had considered the drive from Te Awamutu through Auckland too much of a barrier.

In March 2011, once again we packed up to leave, but while pulling out of the Bay we noticed our neighbours boat had broken its mooring and was washed up on the rocks. Calling out to Luan Nazif, manager of The Beach House next to the Humes, we went closer to their stricken boat only to find it firmly stuck and the seas too big for us to get to it.

There was nothing for it but to drop Luan back on the wharf to do whatever he could, but before leaving I took one last photo - of the empty section beside the Hume property. When we got home I made that photo my screen saver, trying to prolong some of the peacefulness in my heart, before being sucked back into my working life.

But the seed had been sown, and slowly it was about to grow.

We were able to track down the owner of that vacant section, as Dave knew she was from Tauranga, and that she had owned the land for a long time - thirty-six years as it turned out. We managed to track down her brother, and rang him to ask if his sister might possibly be interested in selling. His reply sent my heart racing: "Lady, this could be your lucky day!" He took my details but we heard nothing...

When Dave's only sister, who lives on St Lucia Island in the Caribbean, came to visit us on holiday she became very ill with meningitis, caused by listeria, and had to be hospitalised. While on vigil at her bedside my phone rang. Yes! The owner of the Vivian Bay section was interested in selling and would contact us on her return from an overseas trip.

Our emotions were already strung out, but Dave and I made a pact. Life is short. No matter what the cost, we would follow our dream and follow through, so that we could share this wonderful place at Kawau with our family and friends.

In the hospital waiting room we came across a building magazine, and filled in the long waiting hours making pie-in-the-sky dreams.

Thankfully Sue made a complete recovery, and as I write this she will soon be arriving back on our shores. I am looking forward to showing her in person what she has followed on Skype and from photos over the last few years.

But back to the beginning... It took another six months to finalise the deal, but finally on 30 September 2011, we landed in Vivian Bay, with my first load of plants on board - of course - and sat on our very own land surrounded by boats, timber, and fallen trees. My excitement "runneth over".

It had cost me "an arm and a leg" as Dave and I, for the first time, went half-shares. But there was ample compensation. We were made to feel so welcome by our Vivian Bay neighbours, the Hume family, Luan, Morton's and others that we never felt like 'newbies'.

I overheard Dave telling someone that we would just do nothing for a while, but that was not for me! I would resurrect my old tent that had been around more than a few festivals and campgrounds. Dave knew when to give in.

We bought the emergency depot that had been located on our section to use as a shed, and another emergency depot was erected on the Hume's place. Our shed quickly filled up with tools, locked up for us to use on our monthly visits to clean up the section.

The history of our piece of Vivian Bay soon began to be divulged and I loved every evening when we gathered with neighbours to reminisce about the past. Jan Dickie (nee Morton) remembers as a girl when there were cows being milked and cream being churned into butter. Piers Barney remembers a water-well being dynamited then bricked with rock, by hand. A concrete tank which also stored water for the Bay has become our solar shed. The old green shed that once housed staff working at St Claire Lodge, later housed the wheelbarrows residents used to transport goods from the wharf along the beach to their baches.

We settled on a caravan for our first 'home', and with the help of Johnnie's digger, Chris on the barge, Lyn Hume, Luan, Dave and myself running around with chocks and ropes, it made it up onto our section, never to leave again.

Never mind that we had no power or water. The MacIndoes soon found an old tank, and the Humes ran us a power lead. On the 1st of November we slept our first night on our own place, never mind that the bed was on a lean and we slid down the mattress.

Much against local advice I laid lawn seed. Who would know we were in for a wet summer and soon Dave had to add a lawnmower to his growing number of tools, not to mention his first new chainsaw in thirty years! Now he needed a ute to get all this stuff here. Wasn't that a pity!

In January 2012, our grand-daughters Frida and Cleo arrived. Our first visitors! They had a wonderful time despite the rainy weather every day. After evenings at Cousin Anna's; the children in the hot spa, and the adults with their sundowners (even if the sun didn't shine very much), we carried them home worn out.

My daughter Amy, husband Pat, and their two daughters, Ellie and Celia arrived next. Within a few hours we survived our first accident when Celia fell onto rocks. The sight of blood dripping down her face and all over her Dad's white pants is something I hope I won't see again. Thankfully Patria Hume came to the rescue, patched her up, and the next morning Celia waved good-bye sporting a black eye and a few stitches.

The next arrivals were the Trade Me chipper and dinghy along with Dave's homemade boat-trailer, with his signature stainless steel body, and a trolley for me.

My Christmas presents were never to be the same again.

Back in Te Awamutu my ninety-year-old father, Brian Richardson, was also helping out, searching the garage sales for post-hole diggers and the like, but he outdid himself when he rang me to say he had found a hand-wringer for my washing. I thought that would take a bit of finding. Plans to put a permanent awning and an outside kitchen on the shed were soon put aside as the weather closed in and the caravan became a bit of a catastrophe.

May saw the surveyor arrive to test our house site and with the thumbs up from him we found a plan that fulfilled my wish list, with glass across the front of the house, three bedrooms, two toilets, all under ninety square metres.

Winter fires on the beach got through piles of dead trees and I was surprised how people gathered around enjoying the ambience of the flames, and stoking it just right so that we were only left with embers by sunset.

In August we met the builders, who took us to see their current project in Hideaway Cove. I was amazed how other parts of Kawau were so different, not having ever been further than Vivian Bay. Still I was very happy to get home knowing that, compared to other bays, we only had to carry our barge loads up a small bank above the beach.

Dave and I built new steps up from the southern end of the beach, for people to access the track to Little Vivian Bay and North Cove without walking across our property. Our section had been unused for so long, some people thought it was their right to walk through what would become the middle of our house, so I had to put up a sign to redirect them. One of the first groups to come down the track were heard to say "These people must think they own this track." There was lots of huffing and puffing about it, but now a year on it is accepted as the norm.

Our new build went up very quickly. Starting in April 2013, we surprised anyone who hadn't been into Vivian Bay over the winter months. Dave and I were determined to be a part of it as much as we could, so every barge load saw us onsite keen as to help.

One incident which sticks out was when the anticipated barge arrived with lots of helpers, but only half a load. Apparently the other truckload was booked for the next day, from the same firm.

Someone was going to pay, and it wasn't us!

The builder and his helpers left the Island in disgust because they had run out of framing timber, and the roof trusses due to go up hadn't arrived either. Imagine our surprise when in sails the barge the next day, having arranged to load up on a high tide at Snells Beach. Although we were ecstatic to have our build back on track, as the barge dropped the load on the beach and disappeared, we realised there was only the two of us to get it up onto the building site before the next high tide.

It was a big load. Pallets of timber, roof trusses, the big beam for above the ranch slider, and none of it could stay the night on the beach, so on we slogged. Sometimes I counted how many more loads were left, till Dave shut me up. At least, we thought, Luan would arrive on the 4.30 water taxi, but as luck would have it he missed the taxi, so by the time he arrived after dark there was just the tale to be told, over copious wines.

Luckily when the next barge arrived with the double-glazed windows and doors, Patria had a writing group staying next door, and with help from Luan and anybody else passing by, they were all nailed into place as soon as they were pulled up over the balcony. Our house was taking shape fast.

On the first of July I was a free woman after twenty-five years in retail. While my daughters were young I had started a craft shop with my friend Gail Corboy, along with a wonderful band of other helpers who sold their wares in our shop "Creations" in Te Awamutu. After Kate and Sarah left school I moved to The Mount where we had a holiday home. I had already opened a shop in the main street there called "Uluwatu", as I sourced anything and everything we sold from my twice-yearly trips to Bali.

It was my whole life for the following fifteen years, and I'm grateful for all the support the family gave me. But once I owned my piece of land on Kawau, it was like being back on the farm, gumboots and fresh air. I began to feel trapped behind a counter.

So up went the closing down sign on the shop window. To counteract the trail of people bemoaning another business 'going under' as they presumed, I put up photos of our build in the shop and told them not to feel sorry for me. "I'm off to Kawau Island!" That soon changed the conversation to "Where's that, Waiheke Island?" "Like hell! Think Camp Bentzon and Mansion House."

There was even something in the local paper about me escaping to my private island!

In the July school holidays, Dave decided to have our first sleepover in the house for grand-daughters Frida and Cleo. I don't know who was the most excited, them or us. We carried the mattresses up from the caravan and they never went back down again.

The ceilings had gone up; the kitchen was nearly finished. Sarah and her French boyfriend Geoffroy were the next to stay, and I was in heaven, living onsite, keeping the build on track, while Dave commuted to Te Awamutu.

Dolphins played in the bay frequently over the next few months, spending one whole day mating, rolling onto their backs, and gliding through the shallow waters. I could rattle my bangles and call out, and they would come over to the wharf as if to say hello.

On Labour weekend a large pod stayed in the bay all day delighting anyone who could go out and interact with them on kayaks, paddleboards and dinghies. Any boat arriving in the bay was soon filled with squeals of delight as the dolphins frolicked about their visitors. At the end of the day, from our usual spot on the deck at sunset, we could see them still playing.

It wasn't a hard decision for us to choose solar power. The quote to upgrade and connect to a nearby transformer was crazy, so we tracked down a local contractor for solar power and have been thrilled with our set-up. At first we were cautious about overloading the system but gradually we have introduced more appliances and now I even have a TV and DVD player to get me through the winter nights. A washing machine is waiting to come up.

I'll never want to leave soon.

October saw the last jobs being completed: the "Natural Flow" septic system using tiger worms, the glass around the balcony (which confused the odd weka and seagull), the firebox connected to the hot water cylinder, floors sanded, house painted, and with every trip, more furniture.

Dad found a screen door for the back entrance which lets in the air flow but stops the wekas, mosquitos and blowflies.

Last Christmas saw all our family staying. The house was filled with children, presents, music, good food and nightly games, everything my heart could wish for.

In March 2014 I celebrated my sixtieth birthday and was able to invite all my brothers and sisters, nieces and nephews, along with my friends from the Bay.

Dave has promised to retire next year, after thirty years with Fonterra; then we will start on all the projects next on the list, along with lots of walks, fishing and visitors.

An Island Love Affair

Lynne Banton

An island is a piece of land surrounded by water, so the dictionary states and this is one of the special things about an island, the proximity of the sea. Having lived on an island for most of my life, the ever changing mood of the sea certainly has a reflection on daily life.

I lived on the Channel Island of Guernsey (population about 69,000) for 46 years and my next island living experience (unless you count South Island!) was on tiny Kawau Island (full time population about 40) in the beautiful Hauraki Gulf, both islands being steeped in very different history, but in both cases the sea playing a big part in people and cargo getting transported to and from the islands.

Guernsey Heritage is intrinsically linked to coastal waters; in Roman times Guernsey was a major trading link with Iron Age Britain. Later in the 1800's the Island had over twenty boat building yards producing over 40,000 tons of shipping. The Island's unique position was perfectly placed for both privateering and smuggling. But Guernsey waters take no prisoners and over the centuries a number of ships have met a watery grave around the Island.

Guernsey has a rich history of ship wrecks: I remember a few that have occurred during my life, like on Christmas Day 1973 when the *Elwoodmead*, a brand new ship on its maiden voyage with 125,000 tons of iron ore grounded into rocks. It took 95 days to free this huge vessel. The whole Island went down to have a look at this ship stuck on the rocks, an amazing sight which caused traffic jams in the narrow lanes to the beach with all the 'sticky beakers' wanting to have a look. It must have interrupted many Christmas dinners and had Mum fretting that the turkey would get over cooked!

In January 1974 MV *Prosperity* hit rocks off Perelle and lost all sixteen crew. The ship's cargo was timber which washed up onto the West Coast; I remember the beaches being awash with pieces of timber which we all went to gather up! I bet a lot of that timber was put to use, building garden sheds and such like.

In 1978 the oil drilling rig *Orion* ran aground at Grandes Rocques, the rig which was welded to a barge was being towed, and broke loose in high winds. I remember we could see this in the distance from my Gran and Grampa's bedroom window. It put the thirty three men on board in peril, but all were saved by a dramatic air and sea rescue, some by the skin of their teeth!

The last one I remember was on the 3rd January 2003. (We left in September of this year to come and live in NZ) The *Vermontborg* careered into a reef on the West Coast. The hull was being towed from a builder's yard in Romania to the Netherlands. It broke loose in high winds and became stranded on a reef just yards from the shoreline...another spectacular sight! Nobody was injured, but it was feared that it would be stranded indefinitely with Guernsey's huge tides and it took three attempts before it was pulled free on the 19th January. We were there to watch the freeing process on two of the three attempts, again something

a lot of locals did not want to miss. We took flasks of steaming tea and sandwiches as we watched in cold winter weather in darkness with just the lights from the rescue team, flash lights and torches, to be able to just make out what was happening. We were there on the last attempt and shared the joy and relief everyone felt as she was at last pulled off the reef, free to continue her journey to the Netherlands.

We have a ship wreck museum in Guernsey called "Fort Grey" or as it is known locally the "Cup and Saucer." You can see why it is called this by its shape! It is a Martello Tower built in 1804 to defend Guernsey's West Coast. Many vessels have come to grief on this picturesque but treacherous coast and the Museum houses information panels telling the stories of shipping disasters from 1777 to 2003; it also has a variety of objects recovered from the wrecks.

When we bought our bach in Bon Accord Harbour on Kawau Island, I learnt of very different boats, like the scow, a wooden almost flat bottomed boat designed as a large platform for carrying goods along the coastline and it has been suggested that the efficiency if this coastal transport retarded development of land infrastructure.

In 1880 the scow *Kauri* was wrecked on Kawau Island but the crew were saved and in 1928 another scow *Herald* was ship wrecked at Flat Rock, Kawau Island.

Living on islands we have an abundance of seafood; I was amazed to discover that a seafood delicacy we had in Guernsey, the ormer (*Haliotis tuberculata*) is just like the New Zealand paua. There are three species in New Zealand: *Haliotis iris* (black foot paua), *Haliotis australis* and *Haliotis virginae*.

In Guernsey we can only collect ormers on an 'ormering tide' during the first four months of the year (so the sea is really cold!) on the days around the new and full moons. To collect them legally both feet must be firmly on the sea bed, so gatherers often wear fishing waders to get as far out as possible and turn rocks. No diving is permitted for these creatures as stocks are declining. Some people like to stew, casserole or pickle their ormers. Others beat, slice and roll the pieces in flour and fry them on each side – just like the way Kiwis eat their paua. However Guernsey people have yet to discover an 'ormer fritter' to be on par with the paua fritter!

Both the paua and the ormer shells' inner surface have a layer of iridescent mother of pearl perfect for jewellery making, another 'gem' from the sea.

The older Guernsey generation also liked to stew limpets, the cone shaped shell creatures which cling tightly to rocks, but unless you have the knack of stewing these fishy critters they are like chewing a piece of rubber, not my cup of tea, that's for sure!

On Kawau most residents have a secret spot for collecting mussels. I remember the first time we had our mooring checked by Harry who comes regularly to Kawau Island on his barge, the *Tardis*. He asked me to get a large bucket, which he filled with mussels from our mooring rope that he was inspecting, ooh a lovely feed I thought. But somewhere in the back of my mind I recalled that the mussels needed to soak in fresh sea water for 24 hours to 'spit' any sand out before steaming them open. So I dutifully put the mussels into a nice big bucket of fresh sea water and left them by the back of our property overnight.

In the morning I went to have a look at my mussels only to find that the bucket was nearly empty, where had my supper gone? We eventually discovered mussel shells all the way up our back track, some shells were open and the mussel meat gone, others were still tightly closed. Then a weka poked its head out from the undergrowth; these canny birds had been 'dunking' for the mussels in my bucket, eaten the ones that had opened and were patiently waiting for the closed ones to open up for their next meal!! Kawau Island wekas sure are cheeky birds and clever with it, so after all the effort I reckoned they deserved a feed! We would often see them walking along the rocky Kawau shores looking for small crabs to spear with their rather big beaks. They obviously have adapted well to Island life.

This takes me on to another very different bird also having a distinctive beak that I have come across. Off the coast of Guernsey is Herm Island: permanent population 60 and the island is car free. Around the waters here you will see puffins, black and white birds with big brightly coloured beaks during breeding season. They shed this outer colourful part after breeding. They arrive from the North Atlantic every April to breed in the English Channel and leave around mid-July.

Living on an island you need to grow produce. On Kawau Island large areas were farmed or had orchards providing food for the population. Most of this is now covered in pine trees since Governor Grey's departure and the small population that now live there just have their own little veggie, herb and fruit gardens. Guernsey's horticultural origins go back over 200 years when the first greenhouses were erected. The 'Guernsey Tom' dominated the Island's growing industry throughout the 20th century, with special tomato trains laid on at Southampton and Weymouth to cope with the influx at peak times. Guernsey became a 'glass island' with 7% of its total surface under greenhouses by 1950. Sadly increased competition from Dutch tomato growers and changes in the British railway system eventually made the export of tomatoes less profitable, so Guernsey tomato growers were forced to diversify to grow freesias, roses and clematis.

It's times like this when being an Islander you have to adapt, as although living on an island has its benefits you are still governed by 'the mainland', something Kawau Island is struggling with at present since the Auckland Council spread to make the Super City and included the Rodney District which Kawau came under.

Although Guernsey is governed by "The States of Guernsey" we have the Lieutenant Governor who represents the British monarch. The Bailiwick of Guernsey (which includes the islands of Alderney, Sark, Herm, Jethou and Breqhou) is a British Crown Dependency; the Lieutenant Governor acts as the Head of State and as a liaison between Guernsey and the British Isles.

Mansion House (the former residence of Governor Sir George Grey) on Kawau Island is in public ownership in the Kawau Island Historic Reserve, with strong community support including the Louis Wintle Trust through which some of the current furniture was donated to the house. I was amazed when we first came to live in our bach on Kawau Island and visited Mansion House that this furniture was shipped over from a house in Guernsey; it really is a small world! There is a photo of the house from which the furniture came, but as yet I have been unable to identify the exact house on my birth Island.

On Guernsey we have a famous historic house too, "Hauteville House" which belonged to Victor Hugo and today like Mansion House, it is open to the public from April to September. It was here that Victor Hugo wrote "Les Miserables". We heard very recently that Guernsey is to join a handful of places across the world which have been granted a licence to perform the hit stage show and GADOC (Guernsey Amateur Dramatic and Operatic Club) is the first amateur dramatic society anywhere to be entrusted.

Victor Hugo, the banned poet, left France in 1851 for an exile that lasted nineteen years. Following a short stay in Jersey he came to Guernsey and was captivated by the island. His home, "Hauteville House", in St Peter Port remains today the same as when he left it to return to France in 1870. He wrote "Les Miserables" in 1862 and amongst his other works, "Les Travailleurs de la Mer", (or Toilers of the Sea) the story of which takes place in Guernsey.

Islands always have colourful characters and we were lucky enough to have one living next to us on Kawau Island. Miriam was a wealth of information about the Island having lived there for over thirty-five years. I'd take over some homemade blueberry muffins (her favourite), she'd brew some tea and I'd enjoy listening to her experiences of Kawau life. She loved animals and especially birds. She'd take in any furry or feathery waif or stray, wallaby, weka or whatever! The funniest was a shag which, having fallen from his nest, was found by her son. Shaggy couldn't fish for himself, although he seemed to be a good swimmer, so Miriam would ask me to go and catch a few fish for Shaggy off the end of our jetty. Shaggy would spend a good few hours of the day sitting on Miriam's deck handrail, but as soon as he saw me at the end of our jetty, he'd fly off and over to our jetty steps, walk up them and on to the top and stand by me, waiting for me to reel a fish in!! I had a job to get the fish off the hook fast enough before it was down his throat. One summer Shaggy just didn't turn up. Miriam reckoned he'd passed away. She said he was at least 20 years old so he'd certainly had a good life being hand-fed only the best Kawau Island fish!

In Guernsey there was a colourful chap called Can Can. He always walked with a candy twist walking stick, which he waved in the air and shouted at anyone he didn't like, quite a scary character to me as a young child. He wore a top hat and had a big bushy beard and used to push his tiny little wife around in a pram on the cobbled streets of St Peter Port! Life would be pretty dull without these Islanders.

Since having moved away from Kawau Island to go further north, we are now living by little Motukiore Island which you can only get to when the tide goes down low enough, allowing a passage across the sandy causeway. It is a five hectare recreation reserve with scenic views out to Mount Mania and the Whangarei Heads and features a well preserved Maori Pa; its ancient terraces are still clearly visible.

This is yet another similarity to my years on Guernsey, as there we had little Lihou Island which we could only walk over to at low tide on a rocky causeway for about two weeks in every month. Lihou Island is now an important conservation centre forming a wetland site for the preservation of rare birds and plants. It also has the historic ruins of a twelfth century priory and farmhouse. For a number of years the island had seaweed-eating sheep, so there was no shortage of food for them after a storm! Lihou Island has a "Venus" pool which I used to swim in. It was a big naturally formed rock pool, large enough to swim across. To a child it seemed huge and almost fairy tale like.

Special bonds are formed with people who live on small islands. I think we all enjoy the natural beauty and closeness of nature, walking along tracks, lanes or cliffs, looking at the flora and fauna around us. Making the most of days on the sea, swimming, kayaking, boating and fishing then gathering together and sharing whatever we have made, collected or fished for.

With an island size really doesn't matter! It's the community and richness of people, the history and the scenery...and that is why I have an Island Love Affair.

Visions to Kawau Reality

Ruth MacClement

Kawau was to be a platform suspended in the trees - for a camping pavilion of very moderate proportions.

Look again and you see a fully macrocarpa house - the reality transformed by Gavin.

Tales of solar systems and rhetorical stories of off the grid living ...and now you see a self-made solar system.

I wanted time away and more time to focus on my own thoughts and, with the magic of Gavin; I do live on an island in the trees.

Gavin and I are very different people (sometimes we need to remember that) but we have the happy capacity to follow similar dreams.

Gavin's dreams are squarer, clean lined, solid, with excellent materials and well-proportioned whilst mine are round, made up of a few minimalist sweeps of a charcoal brush and clear of cluttering details - like reality.

We're both stubborn and able to head straight for the goal. We both enjoy simplicity in life, purity in motives and ideas, and deep down quality in people and objects.

Together we make dreams come true.

Looks like we've come to the right place.

Part Three

Somewhere Between Fiction and Fact

Snapshots

Ruth E. Henderson

Flicking the tea-towel, she catches her grandson a beauty and exclaims "You cheeky sausage!" He yelps, shakes the foam off his fingers, and turns to face her. "Gran E, I'm being serious. I need to know about life at the turn of the century." Rolling his eyes, Troy said "If we ever finish these dishes… I'll show you my assignment! "

Troy scrolls through his tablet till he gets to the entry he needs. Thrusting it towards her with a "Gran E, look". She reads 'Year Eight, Term Three, July 2021 assignment – 1000 words - Life at the turn of the century in either a city or an isolated community. Get a first-hand perspective, do not use the internet. Hint - Interview your Grandparents, or Aunties and Uncles, or elderly neighbours.'

A bit indignantly, self-righteously and all in a rush, the youngster blurts out "See! Mum said you lived on Kawau Island before she and Dad got married, before us kids came along. She told me that it was like another world. Very different to Auckland. Backward! No roads, no internet, no cell-phone coverage. Your story must be more interesting than what the other kids will do. You must be able to remember what it was like back then!"

"Oh yes! How could I forget? " Gran leans on the kitchen bench, and starts thinking back to the first year she and her husband Ian lived on the island. Coming out of her reverie, she straightens, absent-mindedly wipes the stove top. "Photos, snapshots, letters…I've still got some, somewhere…you take the dog for a walk...that'll give me time to find my Island Memory Box. Then we can talk."

A little later, settled at the dining room table, as she surveys the pile of photograph prints spread out before them, she looks up absentmindedly and says "What are your brothers up to this weekend?"

"Joel, he's got soccer coaching and is staying at a friend's place. Millen, he's staying with Nana. Mum and Dad don't get back from Hawaii till about 7 o'clock on Monday morning."

"Just as well I've got you for a whole weekend. Every picture here has a story... Give me a moment and I'll sort out the earliest ones."

Lifting up a photo of *Dama*, more of a barge than a boat, she said "This is a good place to begin. To get to the island, you had to travel by boat, maybe not this one, unless you were bringing over some timber and building supplies. *Dama* was a bit different – the local Real Estate Agent, John owned her and he'd bring prospective buyers over in her, use her as other people used a run-about or power-boat. Many times John would pick up your Granddad and me to take us to a friend's place for dinner, or over to Mansion House for a 'do'. You've got to consider that the island had no inter-connecting roads. The only way to get around was to walk, or use a boat of some description. Despite the lack of roads and cars, the island was an incredibly social place. I remember sending a fax to my Mum, your Nana Hills about this..."

Scratching about in her memory box, whilst explaining what a 'fax' was, Gran exclaims..."Golly I've still got it... its dated 14/2/99". She chuckles and reads "Entertained in style last night the friends who helped us move in, with salmon/ avocado/caviar nibbles and olives and smoked mussels for starters, then venison and ostrich fillets with a salad provided by Jill, then fruit salad and coconut cream in parfait glasses with strawberry liquor for half the company and sparkling fruit juice for the other half – provided including the glasses by Merrion. Needless to say much merriment (and for some, wine). I hope I NEVER get over the thrill, amazement and wonder – of all the trouble people go to, to get to places... Jill walked through the mangroves and mud at low tide in her PINK gumboots to John in North Cove, who then took her to Merrion's in Schoolhouse Bay in *Dama* a mini barge, to do some committee business first, then here. Noel rowed up from Stockyard Bay in his tinny. All bringing goods for the evening, or things to exchange, articles for the "Kookaburra", designs for an 'applique' quilt - a present for some long-term but departing residents...then six hours later, doing it all in reverse."

Scanning ahead in the rather chatty fax, she turned to the pile of photos and passed another to Troy, before continuing to read "At midday I paddled over to Mansion House for the George Grey Concert: 'Vocal and instrumental music from the Elizabethan to the Victorian era'. An elderly couple Karen and Leo Cappel played an assortment of hand-made instruments. Autoharp and bowed psalteries the best combo. Others were the gemshorn and autoharp. Held in the courtyard. Historic music in a historic home. How was your Valentine's day weekend?"

"You kayaked to a concert?" "Yes, Troy" she replied. "I used to joke that my kayak was my bike. Even after we got a boat - a 6m Stabicraft - my craft of choice was my kayak. So, if I wanted to go across Bon Accord Harbour, to perhaps collect some pine-cones or to visit Helen for afternoon tea and a slice of her fruit loaf, I'd paddle there. Years later, when we once again lived on the island, I'd even paddle all the way to Sandspit. But in 1999, I didn't know that was possible!

If we wanted to go to town, which was Warkworth, we'd catch either the *Matata* ferry or the *Kawau Kat*. Both ran a regular ferry service from Sandspit, but mid-week or in the winter with only the 10.30 Royal Mail-run sailing, if you had an appointment in the city, or something you couldn't plan for, like a funeral to go to, it could turn into a three day affair. One day to get over, one day for the appointment in the city, and one day to return. For shopping, Friday was the day to go, 'cos then they ran an 'early-off' as we called it and a late afternoon and an evening sailing. You could have a whole day out: do your grocery shopping, take the cat to the vet, get timber or seedlings, or nails or screws for whatever projects you had on the go, have a nice lunch, and then have a lovely chat and gossip on the way home. I tell you, I've never had such a social few years in my life! Once the water taxis took over, it wasn't the same. On the ferry, you could have a beer, and wander about, chat to the 'weekenders' - have Friday drinkie-poohs!"

She pushed another picture towards Troy. "I remember the first few times we came over on the ferry for a long weekend or for Christmas. The stuff people bought with them. It blew my mind. It never ceased to amaze me. Buggies, pet rabbits or guinea pigs, and of course cats, dogs...plants, rolls of netting to put around the trees to keep the wallabies out, new mattresses, kitset shelving, water-blasters, chainsaws, cans of petrol...it was an incredible sight. You have to realise, that everything had to travel by boat. And living on the island, it paid to be organised.

If you got the wrong sized screws or forgot to get the masking tape...you couldn't pop back to the shops the next day. Your project got halted. You had to wait till you went over next, which might be in a fortnight ...or phone a 'weekender' neighbour to see if they could do an errand for you. And if you forgot to buy or ran out of some ingredient when you were making dinner or baking a cake...well, you had to get inventive, you had to improvise."

"Speaking of cake, it's time for supper and soon bed. Be a good lad and stick the jug on and I'll get the cake tin. I'm not boring you Troy, am I?"

"NO, no he beamed... I bet no-one else in class will be getting such interesting stuff!"

Resettled she continued "At every gathering, it was 'ladies a plate'. In other words, bring some food to share. There were no take-aways, no shops, and unless it was a wedding, no catering. So, I had to learn to bake Focaccia bread, Afghans, banana cake... You soon learnt who had which signature or favourite dish that they bought along but it didn't really matter. Pot luck it was. No different from a smorgasbord I suppose."

Spying a couple of favourite pictures, Gran paused, recollecting... looked at her grandson then back at the photograph. Mmm...How to explain this event? There was Merrion clutching her basket, all dressed up in the fur coat that she called 'Fred'.

"John had picked us all up in *Dama*. In this photo we are going ashore in his

dingy, bringing our baskets or dry-bags of food and wine, and dress-up clothes for the night. A lot of times because you were traveling by boat, jumping into dinghies, climbing onto jetties the least you might get was a wet bottom, or if the tide was out and you had to walk in mud, or the tide was high and you had to scramble around rocks or a sea-wall, you could get dirty, so you wore one lot of clothes and your gumboots or reef shoes, to the 'do' then changed in the toilets or someone's spare room." She laughed, "This party was actually a wake, for Noel. He had been an actor, so we dressed up in silly outfits, creating something for fun, from whatever we had in our wardrobes... and celebrated his life in a madcap way, playing "Queen" on the stereo. He would have loved that! 'Who Wants to Live Forever' and 'The Show Must Go On' were played at his funeral."

Whilst explaining what a stereo was, she leaned forward and grabbed another picture. "Oh, here's Noel surrounded by women!

It's midwinter and we're having a mad hatter's party, organised by KIRRA. That's the Resident and Ratepayers Association...they had a 'social committee' and used to send out get well and condolence cards, sometimes flowers, and used to organise a big bash at least once if

not twice a year. I tell you, we might have been isolated from towns and cities, but the island was a party place! We're at Pah Farm. That was a big lodge at the end of Bon Accord Harbour. It had a huge lounge, a big fireplace, a bar, a huge kitchen...perfect for parties, dances, indoor bowls, meetings, training sessions for the First Response Team..."

"What's a First Response Team?" "Questions, questions...enough for now, it's bedtime for you young man. Yes, I know it's not a school night, but it's late and I want to sit here for a bit. Quietly."

Next morning, before she'd even had her first cuppa of the day, Troy swung around on his stool and asked "Gran E, how come you and Poppa went to the island to live, in the first place?"

"Ah ha, maybe I should have started there...Well; it was a bit of a fluke really. We had a plant nursery business at Kaipara Flats, near Warkworth, and one day Poppa came home, with this mischievous grin and a poster folded up in his pocket. Turns out while he was waiting for a chemist prescription he looked in the window of the Real Estate Agent ...and saw this advert for a house, that was on the water's edge, with two acres of native bush, and came with a part share in a jetty, an old dingy with a 2.5hp seagull motor, a sailing dingy, a wind-surfer, and was fully furnished even including bedding, cutlery and crockery. He presented me with the advert, and mused...'You always said you wanted to retire by the sea'. Well, I couldn't believe it...Poppa's initiative! A lady called Margaret was the agent, but she was on holiday. The other agents were obviously reluctant to step on her toes, but we were eager and although it took two weeks, one calm sunny day after agreeing to pay $10 for the petrol, we arrived at the Poplar Bay jetty in the agent's wee run-about.

Once we saw the expansive view, the clear water, the bush, and the open plan house - and had caught our breath...we smiled at each other. This would do us! Of course we didn't tell the agent that...no, we told him we'd think about it. We did, quickly, over lunch at "The Salty Dog"...that was a pub in Snell's Beach... then we marched into their office and signed up, paying the asking price, just like that! Never even considered looking at another place. Mmm...I think they should have given us the $10 back..."

"We used the place as a beach house for eighteen months. We'd roster ourselves off every second weekend - our nursery was a seven day a week business

- catch the 4pm ferry over, blob out, go fishing in the old dingy, potter down to the yacht club – invariably we'd have to clean or change the spark-plug on the old sea-gull motor... Sometimes I'd go over by myself, with just my dog Bonnie. I loved the peace and quiet. One time there was a storm. It was so bad trees fell down and wiped out first the phone line, and then we had a power cut. So, there I was with no lights, no electricity, no phone, so no way of organising a ferry ride out of there – apart from jumping up and down on the jetty and waving madly at a passing boat - and as it was midweek, no neighbours...boy, it was as black as the inside of a cow out there! But the pioneering spirit kicked in...it was like camping in a house. I had candles and could cook on the wood-burner stove and look at the stars, listen to the wind, and just enjoy being.

I was as happy as a pig in mud. Yeah, it didn't take long for the magic of the island to take hold and the idea of living on it full-time to appeal. We got different advice. Old Jean, forever making bonfires, at Stockyard Bay, she told me to go for it, that old age catches you out. But down at the yacht club one day, Ray's girlfriend...she was in her seventies I reckon, told me, don't be in a rush to retire, 'time hangs heavy'."

Helping himself to a second plate of weetbix, Troy settled himself at the luncheon counter and asked "Ok, but, how did you move all your stuff there?" She laughed "It was a bit like a tactical military operation. Rounding up the troops! But first we had to sell our nursery business, which was also our home. So, when we did the two weeks hand-over training we stayed at a Warkworth Motel; Walton Park. Gosh that was hard...going from the country to trying to sleep at a noisy traffic light intersection! Traffic noise is something I loved NOT having on the island."

"Since the beach house came fully-furnished, we had to be very selective in what we packed to take over. There were piles of stuff. Stuff to ditch, stuff to give away, stuff to sell...luckily I had my nephew Aaron staying for the school holidays, helping. The selection process was reduced to three questions. Can I live without this? Ditch or sell. We had a huge 'garage sale' with not just household but farming items. Will I need this if or when we move back to the main-land? Pack to store. We ended up with a whole container of household items, basically a house lot of furniture in storage. And lastly, can I not live without this for two years? Pack to go. That pile was pretty much books, music, paintings, gardening gear, clothes... But we still needed a barge to shift in. That was the first time we fully realised how much we were going to be tide and weather dependent."

Troy wrinkled his brow and interrupted with "What do you mean?"

"Well, the barge could only be loaded at low tide, then had to go across Kawau Bay in calm seas, or else the load could shift and that could be dangerous, or stuff could get wet, and it had to arrive and land and unload at low tide...with an incoming tide, so it didn't get stranded. The first day, we had the van loaded, cars and trailer loaded, a dozen helpers jacked up and it blew and blew. At about 7am we had to call it off. Talk about an anti-climax! But the next day we made it.

Here's a photo of our moving in team...can you spot your Mum and Dad, me and Poppa? The others are Rob, my niece Rachel's boyfriend, Mark, a son of Poppa's friend Wayne, Charles, Len an old friend of Poppa's, and then from the island, Noel, John, Merrion and Reuben. They all deserved a medal. There

was 90 stairs...and since we had a barge going over, we took the opportunity to upgrade the stove, fireplace, washing machine, and thought a deep-freeze would be handy...and they had to be man-handled up. It was a physical day! Speaking of which... today's the day, remember, when I get to choose our activity...and I elect we take Pippa for a big walk! So, you find us a couple of backpacks and I'll throw a picnic together, and we're outta here."

That evening, after dinner, the fire making the place all cosy, dog on mat... the story continued with Troy inadvertently asking the quintessential question islanders get all the time. "But, but what did you do all day?"

She sighed "Ah...On an island, just day to day living takes time! I used to wonder what townies with their mown grass, picket fence, street lights, rubbish bins and houses all in a row did all day!"

Taking a deep breath, she wondered where to begin? Fishing out a photo, and handing it to Troy, with an "All will be revealed!" she ploughed on.

"You've got to understand that just getting groceries, stationary, hardware - by the time you sat on your jetty and waited to catch a ferry till you got your groceries in the door...it took a whole day...it was not like in city where you can get them delivered to your door or you hop in the car, drive to the supermarket and drive into your garage, and carry a few bags indoors....I counted up the number of times we had to handle groceries to get them into our kitchen - after we'd paid for them and they were in the supermarket trolley. Seven times! Trolley to car, car to wharf, wharf to ferry, ferry to jetty, jetty to wheelbarrow, wheelbarrow to foot of the stairs, then backpack or carry bags up 90 steps. So, shopping, that took time."

Taking all this in, working it out Troy asked "So, this was, what, once a week! What happened if you ran out of something?"

"One of us usually went over once a week or ten days. There was no corner diary, no supermarket...you had to be organised. We used to have an exercise book. If you opened a new bag of sugar or flour... then you wrote it down on your list...for the next time you went to town. If you were desperate, the yacht club did have some bare essentials, like tinned food, detergent, crackers and biscuits. They only had fresh stuff and refrigerated things at Christmas time. Prices were about double town prices, so were only for those desperate or reckless with their money."

Tapping the photo she held, she reflected "On this occasion Poppa's cousin Florence was over from Melbourne, so we've got more than just groceries. That old backpack...my Mum and Dad gave me that for my 20th birthday" she beamed. "It's been all around the world...your Uncle used to laugh about it... and even offered to buy me a new one...but it was just perfect for carting stuff. Food up the hill and firewood down. You always tried to avoid going anywhere empty handed. Pebbles and shells for the pathway, seaweed for the garden went up...bucket by bucket building up the pathways or building up the soil. But I'm getting ahead of myself. Steps up the hill and a garden came later. "

"Initially, we needed to settle in and get the house the way we wanted it. Our van and ute had been sold with the business, so first off we had to buy a car. We wanted a 'bomb', nothing too flash as it would get rusty parked at Sandspit... we picked up this 1977 Mitsubishi, from the side of the road, for $600 and it ran like a charm. We never spent a penny on it. It was a fun set of wheels; we called it "Kermit" after the frog in the "Muppets". It was actually greener than the photos show. The passenger window was wedged shut with a bit of cardboard, if it rained, you had to mop up the dashboard with a towel.

We carted stuff on the roof, poking out of the boot...that old hat stand, bits of furniture... There was no "Trade Me" then....so we spent a few days fossicking around in Auckland's second hand shops and had a china cabinet and Poppa's desk delivered to our jetty on the *Kawau Kat*. From there Poppa and I wheelbarrowed them along the beach.

To get them up the hill we'd enlisted young Reuben to help. He came after dinner. The desk went up fine, but by the time it was the china cabinet's turn it was practically dark. On the first landing Poppa lost his footing...he was the guy going up backwards. He fell down the bank onto my kayak. Dear Reuben wrapped his arms around that piece of furniture and lugged it up by himself!

Later on, sitting at the table, Poppa felt something warm on his leg. When I saw what it was, I admit I swore. Blood and a 50mm gash on his shin that went right to the bone! It was a neat and tidy wound, but really needed stiches... If I was in town, I'd have been driving right then to the emergency clinic. But flipping heck, we were on an island and it was then about 9pm. Too late to call

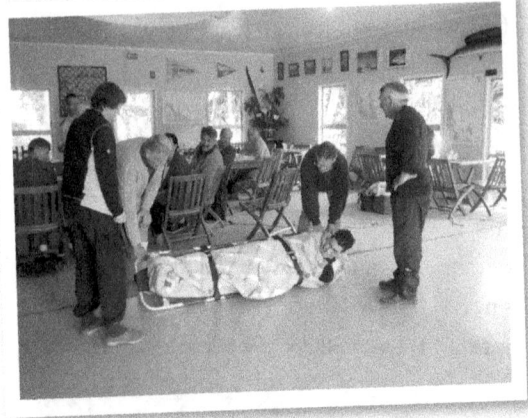

for help unless it was a real emergency. So, I got out the Dettol and swabbed it clean, and pulled the shin together using the wound closure method, but not having any steri-strips, I cut up strips of adhesive tape. That was the first time I felt a bit vulnerable on the island. But actually we were well cared for, medically… which brings me to the First Response team".

Seemingly forever hungry Troy piped up "Can we have a bit of your apple cake and a milo first?"

The boy and the fire refuelled, Gran passed a photo to Troy and carried on "When I joined the Fire team it was also locally called the First Response or Rapid Response team. We responded to any emergency. We met every month for a training day – fire pumps to first aid."

Glancing at the photo, she said "That was actually a weekend first aid course at Pah Farm. Compared to how the Kawau Island Volunteer Fire Force developed, back then it was a bit of a 'Dad's Army'. We didn't have a siren or pagers or even have proper uniforms, let alone a rapid response vessel and it was a bit sexist! We girls operated the phones…had a telephone tree."

Troy raised a quizzical eyebrow. "This was before cellphones and texting…we rang around… rounding everyone up! Fire comms rang the Fire Chief Kevin, who then rang say Jill or Linda who rang me or Merrion. Then Jill (or Linda, whoever was home) rang Don who had a big fast boat called *Double Trouble*, then the other fire-fighters in North Cove while Merrion or I then rang folk in South Cove and Bon Accord. And if it was a serious job, the plan was to go over to Mansion House, where there was a VHF radio."

"Fire was, still is, the island's worst enemy, its greatest danger! The main jobs were first aid. Thank goodness! We girls were allowed to do medical stuff. If it was minor, like a broken arm, then we'd bandage the patient up and put them on Don's boat and off they'd go with someone to drive them to the Doctors or the hospital on the mainland. If it was a bit more serious, we'd arrange to have an ambulance meet us at Sandspit and if it was really bad, really urgent, like a heart attack then we'd call up the helicopter. So, we weren't totally in the back-blocks. We reckoned we could get a patient into hospital faster than someone in the suburbs!

Troy all serious, on a fact-fining mission piped up "So, how many people actually lived on the island at the turn of the century?"

"Oh, the number bandied about was usually 90. That's full-timers. Even if you lived there for a week or three at a time, if you had a house on the mainland you were not included in the count. In the holiday season the floating population... people on yachts or launches plus in the 300 odd baches....well, then we estimated we had two or three thousand extra people – who were liable to do silly things like get out of a dingy at low tide and stand on a stingray or get lost in the bush or set off firecrackers or flares into the bush on New Year's Eve. So, one way or another we were kept busy or on high alert at those peak times."

"What about to your place, did you get many visitors?"

"Yeah!!! Did we ever! We were a novelty, the place to go to for those two years. Here, you look at the entries in our visitor's book for 1999. Count the signatures. Troy applied himself to the task and told her "72"

"That's a staggering number. Mind you, they didn't all sleep the night; some came on yachts, anchored in our bay, and came ashore for a shower and a shared dinner or just for a leg stretch and morning tea.

Then in winter we had the place all to ourselves."

Nodding her head, Gran said "That question, 'What did we do all day?' Well, with or without guests, there was always walking the dog and exploring, my favourite pastime." Reclaiming the visitors book Gran looked for her friend Suzanne's 1999 entry and read out "Walks with Ruth should be mandatory," and below that from Jan S. "Walks with Ruth should be definitely banned" and soon after, Wayne's "We survived Mt Taylor..." She laughed. "I was a bit, just a tiny bit mean... most city folk found the hills...challenging."

"My main walking mates lived on the island...there was my neighbour Noel who'd talk the leg off an iron pot. He was so entertaining and used to skite that in his London days he'd met the 1960's pop group the Beatles. Then there was Helen from Swansea, famous for her gorgeous psychedelic hand- knitted sweaters,

Tessa from Karaka Bay, John's son Thomas who was on Correspondence School lessons, and Jill the cartoonist Sam's daughter, both from North Cove. Noel and I would meet 'one o'clock at the top of the hill'.

Not long after I arrived, it was he and I who put tags on the trees marking the way from the big cairn above the yacht club to Mt Taylor. I called on Helen, who had been scrambling around the island for years to help Thomas and me to mark the track from Mt Taylor past the old sledge to the Old Coach Road which went all the way to the top of Rocky, then to Vivian Bay in one direction and in the other out, to Smugglers. We used torn up tea towels or shopping bags, but over the years switched to using cut

up strips from yellow plastic potting mix bags. Not everyone approved... but I tell you what, a hell of a lot of people soon used 'our' tracks...and I heard of many who were pleased not to be 'fumbling around in the dark, lost'."

"We had some grand days! We all had dogs. I recall one day at Rocky Bay – we had dog races. Noel, Jill's son and Thomas holding on to our pooches, with me and Jill at the finish line scratched in the sand – yelling, screaming, leaping up and down, encouraging our dogs to run their little hearts out. Jill's dog, a fox terrier usually won. On the weekends and holidays my neighbour Sue would turn up with Chloe, her Airedale terrier and we'd go walking, or fishing or play petanque. Her partner Terry was a nutter on it, they had their own court, and he went overseas to tournaments. We'd have Shirley and John, and Chic and Brian from North Cove around and have our own tournaments. Talk about laugh...oh, sunny summer days. Look there's Polly, Chic's dog."

"Sometimes, I walked not just for fun or exercise but with a purpose. As a delivery girl. For a while I was the Secretary for KIRRA, the residents and ratepayers association, so I'd get the mail...once a week in a big sack or mailbag off the ferry, but need to get some of it to the Treasurer. That was John, and at the time he did odd jobs about the island, so I'd find out where he was working and then kayak or walk to transfer the mail. I could have posted it to him, but that would mean a two week delay in him getting it...by the time the mail went back to the city and them came back in his mailbag. I'd also walk to committee meetings with Tessa. She home schooled her youngest son Cam - often seen in atrocious weather up the harbour mastering his sailing skills in his P class...he went on be a world class sailor.

Anyway, Tessa, she'd have rowed over from Karaka Bay on the opposite side of the harbour - we'd meet at the big cairn and we'd walk over to Vivian Bay, spend however many hours the business took, then walk and or row home. Maybe four hours of business and four hours of travel...and you ask what we did all day!"

"The island's three monthly magazine the "Kookaburra", also had its 'headquarters' at Vivian Bay - and there Gael, Lyn, Linda, Jill and sometimes others, beavered away typing up other peoples contributions, editing, proofing, then literally pasting up the magazine. In those early days when hardly anyone had a home computer, to' Cut and Paste' meant using scissors and glue! So... that was another excuse to go for a walk - to hand deliver stories or meeting minutes for publication, this was, before we got on email.

Pulling out another photo and plonking it on the top of the growing pile, she beamed at her grandson.

"Can you believe that? We had fried fish for breakfast, hot smoked fish with garden fresh salad for lunch, fish pie for dinner and guests could take some home. We worked our way through Alison Holst's 'Meals without Red Meat' recipes. The limit then was nine snapper per fisherperson per day and the size restriction was 27cm!

We never got 'a bin full' but we sometimes did get our limit.

Your Mum was a keen fisherwoman! If it was too rough to go out in Babe our boat, we'd surf cast off the jetty. Often Sue, would spy us over her lavender hedge, and come out to join us, with her hand-line. I'd be the big show off, swishing my line way over her head out into the bay, and she'd sit there on the jetty steps, smirking, pulling in her dinner!"

Muttering to herself, Gran scratched around in the bottom of the box, and held aloft a letter. "I thought I'd kept it. It's a carbon copy of a newsy letter I wrote to Suzanne, dated 29 July 1999....describing life on the island, before she visited us. My peripatetic pen-pal was living in Vietnam at the time." Distractedly, she continued "its four pages long...you have a shower and get ready for bed..."

Ten minutes later, still engrossed, Gran tapped her finger on the first page and excitedly said "Troy, you must listen to this bit... "Soon to be developed will be a shot of me holding up two kingfish.'"

Anticipating Troy's question she looked up and explained "Cameras used film - it wasn't instant, you had to be patient, take your roll of undeveloped film into the chemist and come back a week later to get your prints! I didn't get my first digital camera till Christmas 1999 and at that time, as well as my wee Ricoh 'point and shoot' also used a bulky SLR Minolta film camera with telephoto and close up lenses! One day I'll take you to MOTAT and show you typewriters that used carbon paper, cameras that used film, fax machines, stereos ... meanwhile I'll read on."

"'We landed one each and lost four or five each. But oh what a magical day's fishing that was. It was low tide, bright and sunny...not usually the most successful of conditions. Well, we were at one of our favourite spots, Pembles Island, just enjoying the sunshine. I put a punctured milk bottle of burley (we make our own from fish guts, pig or goat feed pellets and smelly tuna oil) down the anchor chain...and suddenly we were in an open sea aquarium...could see all the action...sprats, kingies, John Dory all zipping about. Any scraps we tossed over the side, the kingies zoomed in for, but they ignored even the juiciest bait 'sandwich' so we decided to try and trick them into thinking our baited hooks were free floating or live. It worked. We have since looked up 'the book' and indeed we were lucky as they only take live bait or lures that you jig. Our usual haul is snapper, but I can recommend smoked kingfish. It's as tasty as salmon'."

Putting the letter aside Gran said "Yeah, we had a lot of fun in that boat. My Mum ingrained in us girls the 'girls can do anything' philosophy...taught us to change spark plugs and to fillet fish and the boys to iron and sew on buttons! When Poppa and I went out in our boat, on the way out he'd be the skipper and I'd be the deckie, then unlike some couples, we'd reverse roles on the way home...he'd lift the anchor, I'd drive, drop off any passengers at the jetty, he'd grab the buoy, then we'd row ashore in our 'rubber ducky'. Then Poppa would leave me to clean or fillet the fish!"

Lost in thought Gran shuffled a few photos around, until she found the one she was after.

"This was taken at a fishing contest...not the famous "Furuno" – that was for super serious chaps, about 3000 of them would flock down to Pah Farm at the end of the harbour, get on the booze, then zoom out at about 5am and in again at about 3pm for the weigh in...we saw some big momma's there – we'd go down for a decko; 10kg was not uncommon. No, this was a local casual contest. Tessa, Sue and I teamed up and adding an 's' to the boats name we called ourselves the 'Babes' team. Can't remember what we caught, but do recall we fished off from the Thornton Light at the northern tip of the island, in crystal clear waters and out at Maori rock in the channel between the island and Tawharanui Peninsula. Before it was a sanctuary!"

"That boat was a beaut. It was designed to take on the Foveaux Strait, and theoretically could have six big scuba divers and tanks standing on one side and

still be stable. So, we had faith in her...but we'd still take heed of the weather forecast. We didn't just go fishing in her...we'd go visiting, even go to vote!"

Catching the raised eyebrow, she said "Yeah, it's hard to believe nowadays, but back then, you had to physically go to a polling booth, and put your mark on a piece of paper... and Kawau was no different ...except of course that we didn't drive there or catch a bus to the booth, we went by boat to our booth at Camp Bentzon..

I'd use her to take people to "Bookworms", our book club. It was called Island Readers then. We'd meet in a different home in a different cove or bay each time, bring a plate for afternoon tea, and talk about two or three books we'd read, and maybe swap or borrow each other's. It was a social gathering, a catch up on local gossip... One month I'd go around Bon Accord in *Babe* picking up people and the next month Tessa would pick us up in her run-about. Or if the weather was too foul to get out into Kawau Bay, we'd walk ...maybe over the hill to the sheltered North Cove and then someone would pick us up in their dingy so we could get up Moana Creek or to wherever the meeting was. There was always a way to get to where you wanted to go, even if it was the long way."

"Time took on a different meaning on the island. In fact the first of the Kawau Commandments was 'Throw away your watch'.

"Commandments? Troy quizzed.

"Yep, Commandments. Like the Ten Commandments...but rather than 'Thou shalt not, it was more like Thou shall! Over a period of a few months (and probably a few drinks...) a few of us faxed ideas back and forth on what 'rules' we should have. Not mainland rules! And not children's rules! They were simple to start with, but then over the months they got crafted and polished and added to. We certainly ended up with more than ten." Delving deep into her treasure box she exclaimed "Here... Here we go... "'Throw away your watch, your inhibitions, and most of your possessions.'" Scanning ahead to 'Dress the way you want to (with or without knickers).' She said "You're a bit young to understand all of these...but have a look. And now, I think we should abide by rule three."

After a few minutes Troy looked up saying "I like number three, 'Make time for play and time for dreaming'."

"So do I! Off to bed now...sweet dreams... have you decided what you want to do tomorrow? Is it to be the Planetarium or the Leonardo de Vinci expo at the Museum or do you have another idea?"

After a yet another full day on her feet, Gran sat rubbing her sore foot, the fire making the room all cosy, chocolate biscuits and milo ready for later, and mused... "It's hard to comprehend how much was unknown in de Vinci's time, how ahead of his peers in his thinking he was, but you know what, at the turn of the century we were ignorant of many things too. Have you ever heard of the 'Y2K' bug? No? Well, listen up! 'Y2K' was shorthand or texting for Year Two Thousand.

We were all brain washed - not just Islanders, not just New Zealanders, but everybody, everywhere - that if the world didn't end as the clock struck midnight on 1.1.00 well, everything to do with computers from air-traffic control to cash registers would go haywire. Gloom merchants had everyone believe that things electronic, even electric would all cease to work as we went from '99 to '00. Shops sold out of bottled water, torches and batteries, tinned food, candles... Anyway on that night, your Aunt, Dad, Mum, and two of her friends, Nicole and Karen were all here to party and stayed the night. Poppa and I were 'on duty' till midnight, he was involved with Civil Defence and I with the Fire Team. Lucky for us - it was a rainy night, and that not only reduced the fire risk, but dampened spirits and the number of idiots letting off fireworks or rowing about in the dark, and falling in the tide as they climbed aboard neighbouring yachts. We watched that clock, waited and waited...not really knowing what to expect... would the 'Y2K' bug get us?"

"Once the clock stuck 12, and the power was still on, and there was no apparent emergency, Poppa and I had a drink or two...we had some catching up to do. Previously I'd thought I'd make the pilgrimage up to Mt Taylor in the pre-dawn to see the first rays of the new millennium in, up there. So, I'd set my alarm clock. We didn't fall into bed...couches, mattress's ...everywhere, till I don't know, about 2am, but I was still keen on the plan, then. That was till the damn thing on my bedside table went off at about 5am. I turned it off, but damn, it kept going...I ended up smashing the bloody thing against the wall! And still it kept going. Was it the 'Y2K' bug? No. Your Mum walked up the stairs and without a word, turned off the second alarm clock on a chest of drawers. Here... read your Dad's entry in the visitor's book."

Troy's wide eyes changed to a puzzled expression as he read "'31.12.99 - 01.01.00 Happy Wai toe kay. Thanks for the great night. Civil Defence ok. Computer ok. Toaster ok. The only problem was suffered by the alarm clock. Never mind. Hope the next millennium brings more happiness and joy for you both.'"

"Oh, I get it Y 2 K!"

"Yes. So, after all the fuss, the world carried on, much the same as before. The only tricky thing was knowing how to say the year. In 1999, you'd talk about what happened in '87 or '98 but in 2000 we didn't know what to say. So for at least that year, most people said in full, 'two thousand' or 'the year 2000' rather than nought nought or O O or zero zero. Later on as the century progressed we'd say O one or O eight...the year you were born!"

"In the New Year we had a big party at Camp Bentzon in North Cove - the Millennium Ball. Most of the island was there...we dressed the main hall up, typical kiwi style with fern fronds and balloons, had a band...had a ball, you might say. Some of the 'girls' had rehearsed a song and dance routine - 'New York New York' a stage show number of Liza Minnelli's. It went down a treat. Yet another top night! Here's a photo of some of the troupe coming onto the stage..."

Gran shuffled the last few photos around, plucked one out and plonked it down. " You've got school tomorrow and this photo is a good one to end this story on...We made our own fun...

this was Poppa's birthday and we had friends around for an Indian style dinner, and dressed up, as best we could in 'Indian' clothes."

She chuckled "I'm actually wearing a sarong and cotton top that I bought in 1975 when I travelled around India with Suzanne...I still have the sarong!

Anyway...as the night wore on..." her eyes lighted on the Kawau Commandments: "Number 9 - 'listen to your music lots and as loud as you want' came into force.

We used carrots, parsnips, and spoons as microphones and let rip! We sang our hearts out. It was a hoot! Oh it was a fun night. We had so many of those on the island! It was all about good friends really - or making friends, being friends with whoever lived near. A sister-in-law gave me a card once, which I kept; with the saying 'Happiness is the art of making a bouquet of those flowers within reach.' I'd say that pretty much sums up Kawau. You end up living amongst some interesting, exotic, wonderful, wild and wacky bunches of flowers or groups of people! Salts of the earth; spices of the world!"

"I'm forever glad we sold our business, jumped off the deep end and had two years of 'early retirement' on Kawau...

One of my favourite books is a true story by Susan Duncan, "Salvation Creek". In it she says 'The greatest risk in life is not to take a risk. Sometimes you have to risk everything to find the only thing you need.' "

"Kawau gave me everything I needed."

Troy B. July 2021 Year eight assignment

Life at the turn of the century in an isolated community

In January 1999 my Grandmother and Grandfather Henderson moved to live on a tiny island in the Hauraki Gulf. The island is called Kawau. It is 65 km by road north of Auckland's harbour bridge and about 10 km by sea from Sandspit. This is my Gran E's story.

Nelson Girls: a Dog's Tale

Jen Seel and Jenny Spring

Outside the winds were howling, the rain was drumming against the windows and as often happens, after a couple of flickers, the power failed. Not that I worry much about this, I love it. It means the fire will be lit, and I won't have to go for a walk. When I can't hang on any longer, I pace up and down near the door and Jen or Jen will let me out to nip up the path to do my business. Then a hasty retreat back to the fire. My kind of life.

Jen and Jen (they're my owners) were reflecting about how I came to be their dog. It all started when their Auckland neighbour, Jean, died. She had a dog called Artie and they had known him since he was a pup. They decided to be Artie's new owners. No small responsibility as Artie, by then thirteen years old, was an Irish wolfhound about the size of a truck. Kawau was their home, so after Jean's funeral, they collected their new charge, settled the check-up bill with the vet, picked up his bedding and toys and drove him to Sandspit.

I overheard them once discussing the number of handlings required to move something from the mainland to the island. The list looked something like this:

1. Loading article(s) in the mainland vehicle
2. Unloading from that vehicle onto wharf at Sandspit
3. Carrying everything onto ferry or water taxi
4. Offloading from ferry or taxi onto Schoolhouse Bay wharf
5. Transporting along the wharf in a trolley

6. Loading all into Kawau vehicle for drive up Schoolhouse Bay Road
7. Unloading vehicle when parked on property
8. Carrying everything down steps into house
9. Unpacking and putting away.

Artie completed all of the above procedures, even walking the distance between steps 6 and 7. I can tell you that thirteen years old is getting on a bit for an Irish wolfhound. Artie had been in kennel accommodation for weeks, his owner and best mate wasn't around anymore, and he didn't really know where he was.

I'm not surprised that Artie was not interested in the dinner placed in front of him. He just sighed and settled himself down in the space between the stove and the fridge which meant that everyone had to step over him if they wanted to get into the bedroom. All sorts of cajoling, loving hugs and toy shaking was trialled, but nothing got him to move. A few hours later he shut his eyes, put his head to the side and quietly doffed his mortal coil.

Many tears followed the phone calls imparting the news of Artie's demise. The owner of the dog kennels, an obvious believer in getting back on a horse after falling off, offered to sell the Jens a new born Old English sheepdog for $800 (that was ME!!!). Unfortunately they were still reeling from Artie's vet fees, so declined the offer. I was purchased by another couple and whisked off to live in a house in Pakuranga.

Back to Artie. What to do with a dead dog the size of a small horse lying in between two essential kitchen appliances and the bedroom door? Being resourceful souls, Jen and Jen sent out an invitation to neighbours and a resident DOC ranger - "come for dinner, bring your shovels".

The burial hole was dug as deep as the dry clay would allow and, with two diggers taking two legs each, Artie was laid ceremoniously to rest in the north-west corner of the section between a couple of olive trees. His toys and bedding were buried with him along with a photo of his late caregiver to comfort him on his way.

More tears were shed. The neighbours and the DOC ranger raised their glasses to toast Artie's brief time on the island. It was after the third or fourth toast that the idea was mooted that Artie's gravesite would be the ideal place for a chicken coop. To clinch the deal it was realised it would also serve the purpose of stopping the wekas digging him up.

Before the chook house construction could get underway, the kennel owner rang to say that I was back on the market as I kept on making the Pakuranga couple sneeze. Between you and me I don't think that was the case at all, they probably realised I was going to cost a bit to feed. The previous $800 price tag was to be reduced by $600 – I was a steal. The kennel owner had to admit that I was the runt of the litter, had stopped breathing shortly after birth, been revived by mouth to mouth. In addition a few imperfections had come to light. I had a wall eye that didn't function too well, a deaf ear that didn't function at all, hip dysplasia and one testicle - how embarrassing! The Jens also had to promise not to turn me into a show dog. Fat chance!

With confidence that attending dog shows would unlikely to be a temptation, a short memory about their recent very brief dog ownership experience, and one Jen also being the owner of a non- functioning ear, Jen and Jen said they'd love to welcome me to their household. I was to be collected in a few weeks' time, once the change of ownership processes had been completed. Makes me sound like a car.

This gave time for the chook house edifice to emerge from a pile of scavenged material, wood off cuts, and chicken wire. It was an impressive structure, with slat louvered ventilation, bark stripped manuka perches, and laying boxes with external hinged doors. The nor-west corner was fenced off and an impressive commemorative sign, ARTIE'S HEN HOUSE, was painted and nailed over the coop door.

Now for some chooks. An advertisement in the Rodney Times announced red shavers, good layers, for sale in Wellsford. Within a week the nine step process was underway again, this time with five hens in ventilated cartons and me, a little twelve week old ball of black and white fluff on a lead. I may have had some physical and sensory imperfections, but I had a lofty pedigree. My impressive moniker was *Lord Nelson of Snowdragon*. I think this may have been a homage to my historic name sake who also was a bit one eyed.

Somewhere between steps 3 and 4 two of the hens laid an egg each, an encouraging endorsement to the wisdom of this launch into the poultry venture. And I, Lord Nelson of Snowdragon, had become just plain Nelson, occasionally even Nellie when I had been especially cute.

I have to say that right from the start I had a bond with those five feathered girls. I guess being in close confinement on a sea voyage does that sort of thing. The hens became known as Nelson girls. I was disappointed though when I could see that a definite pecking order was developing in their ranks. Jen and Jen had christened the flock in honour of their mothers' dead friends - Pam, Tui, Peg, Zoe and Thelma. Pam quickly declared herself the matriarch of the flock and poor Thelma's feathers were destined to never stand a chance.

For the next two years I kept an eye on my girls as they pecked around the garden. Pam and her entourage gifted Jen and Jen with two to three eggs a day, a weed free section and heaps of fertiliser from the weekly hen house clean. I contributed too, mostly in the fertiliser department, and ensuring my owners had a twice daily walk even when it was raining.

By the time our time on Kawau was coming to an end the laying prowess of Pam and her entourage was common knowledge in the neighbourhood. My humans were not surprised when the couple living up the hill said they would not only take the chooks off our hands, but would also take their beautifully built "Artie's Hen House" residence

I overheard days of discussion of the logistics of moving this well built two metre cubed wooden structure up a 30 degree slope to a quad bike and waiting trailer. The deliberators were three chaps who lived in our "hood". Between them they had a wide set of skill sets. One had childhood memories of survival in Holland during World War II and had built and sailed his own yacht in New Zealand waters. Another was a good kiwi number eight wire bloke and very handy with a chain saw. Number three, like me was mindful of his physical limitations, and was ever so generous in the amount of advice he was willing to offer.

The chainsaw man soon made short work of the foundations, the yacht builder rigged up a series of ropes and pulleys and, slowly and surely, the hen house moved up the slope. I watched all this with bated breath, while Jen and Jen and a few other neighbours followed proceedings with much amusement and comments. A sharp cry and some gasps of horror alerted me to something amiss, so I barked and ran in circles to make sure everyone knew there was an alarm on. A rope had got caught round number three's artificial leg and loosened the straps that kept it in place. The leg took off down the slope and I was all prepared to go and fetch it back for him but one of the Jens held my collar. As the leg started rolling down the slope and its owner started to topple, chainsaw man assessed the situation. In a flash he had calculated the length of number three's good leg, the length of what was left of the not so good leg and the hypotenuse of the gradient between. Realising that he was in the worst possible position he swung his teetering mate 180 degrees so he was standing up straight on the slope. What an achievement, and a grateful thumbs up from number three. There was a down side though, number three couldn't move from this position. Like a trooper he kept up his good advice until the hen house was secure on the trailer and his wayward leg had been retrieved by someone else from under a grape vine.

After a celebratory beer or two and a plate of homemade shortbread, ARTIE'S HEN HOUSE and its occupants were waved off to their new home up the hill. The fencing in the North-West corner was removed and the olive trees left to flourish in the well fertilised soil. An old dinghy serving as a flower bed was put in place over Artie's grave and, not to be wasted, the ARTIE'S HEN HOUSE sign was tacked over the entry to the workshop.

I missed my girls. Each evening after I had done my "busy-busy" I wandered over to the north-west section to have a good sniff and reminisce of the good times we had. I sometimes lay down next to the old dinghy to chat with Artie and thank him for the part he played in bringing me to this magical island.

I'm still here you know. My ashes are scattered in a most fitting place, in the cemetery on the hill. As for my girls, they named a rose in their honour, NELSON GIRLS. The Jens planted one by the dinghy in the north-west corner.

Woof!

Tide Talk

Jane Myhre

There you are again. Our daily communion. How many years has it been? In your human scale, many. In earth terms, a mere tick.

At first I felt your gaze as a question. But what can I tell you?

I am rock and clay, sand and shell. Stalk, trunk and leaf bristle from my slopes. Around me tides go out and come in again, as they do around the larger mass you inhabit. Above us both, sun and moon track east – west. That is all there is, I would have told you, should you have demanded I respond, should I have been miraculously gifted with speech.

These you can depend upon. Wordless rush of the sea following the white orb. Warm benevolence of the golden orb rising from the darkness. Cadences of wind.

Today my thoughts reach you by way of a westerly. My thoughts? Perhaps more what you humans call feelings. Whatever, the communication between you and I has no articulation, no sound.

Conversely, you humans never cease to chatter. Scattering your thoughts wherever you go, words flying through the air, seeding desire, need, direction, all-conquering across the innocent earth.

Forgive me. I am being unkind. You cannot be otherwise. And, generally speaking, I like visitors of your kind.

Eagerly they arrive, tickling me, digging their toes in. Warm sand brings a smile to their faces, always. I do bring pleasure, no question about that.

But as you have observed, access is a tad tricky. Requires expertise. Only one approach is possible: there, between two reefs, there, where the sand drapes down to the water, an apron to cling to. Down clatters the anchor.

Some are deterred, thank goodness. Please don't be offended, but I don't want to be overrun by your species.

Most human visitors walk all the way around me soon after arrival. Curious lot aren't you. What is on the other side? No, not paradise. Pretty much like the side they landed on, though shadier. Still, I sense it is with some feeling of achievement, perhaps relief, to find themselves soon back where they started.

We can see a dinghy coming in now, you and I. I feel the little ripples as they row in; you up there on top of the ridge reach for your binoculars.

You and I both know the routine: sifting sand through fingers, sprawling to look up at cloud and sky, legs arcing. I grant you it must be wonderful to *move*. Still, I have movement all about me.

The winged ones, swooping, fluttering, crying out. Tiny quick insects scrambling under rocks, amongst grasses, lurking in rotten wood; or, wary, despite their shelly defences, of the stalking herons, crustaceans edging about my rocky crevices.

And as I can see my visitors have judged the gap in my reef rightly. While they are pulling their dinghy up onto my beach, I shall go on. Beneath my skirts glide many delightful creatures having fins or tentacles, nudging into my cavities, tugging at the weed sprouting from my nether parts, somersaulting in the coming and going of the water. Yes, all this movement is spirit enough.

I think you can see the sign (it will rot in time) which pierces where the bulk of me rises from my sandy apron. It designates me a 'protected area'. That you humans might protect me is ludicrously arrogant, as I understand the scheme of things, but touching.

What is safe? No creature, no place. What is lasting? Earth, water. Darkness and light.

Even I cannot escape change. Long before you humans sprang down from the trees and invented language, (for which thanks) I emerged from the centre of myself in a massive spurt of flame - volcano to be precise - and no doubt will return in some future tremor.

But here, now, I am hardened, unmovable. For the most part. I do slip and leak a little round the edges, but that is little matter. Proud, seasoned. In places, I admit, striated, even prone to fracture where wind or rain pierce my outer skin. I see your wrinkles. You know what I mean.

Ah, the dinghy is now well above the high tide mark. Several humans ashore. Skipping about as if they owned me!

Did you see that? One of them has pulled out the sign! What a relief. As I said it had been irritating me. A thorn in my side, I believe you might say.

Now look at this. Can't help themselves can they? Tugging, pulling themselves up my body by branch and by twig. Kicking their feet into my steepness. Such spirit! Determination and a bit of luck might get them to my peak. But I doubt it. Typical of you humans. The need to climb, to conquer. Can you see the pebbles sliding down to the beach as they struggle, grab, kick their way up? It doesn't hurt me, but it is a loss.

You will be watching them.

***

Ten years have passed since I first arrived here, and yes, I do look at you every day, usually in the evening.

This is interesting. Not many head straight for the top as soon as they arrive. Ooooops one has slipped. No, saved himself just in time. Crawling up again. Steep there. The conquering spirit.

Gulls everywhere. Swirling above the channel, lurid green, as the sea often is in a westerly tracking south. No, I don't have a question for you. At the end of the day it is restful to gaze upon the sea, my thoughts darkly floating, like the shadows of the tall pines on my side of the channel. Rock, water, cloud.

I've gotten to know the sea's palette over the years. On a calm midday, blue, like the Madonna's cloak. Later, pewter as the sun slips behind the peninsula sprinkling gold in the dimpled tide.

Whoops, he's slipped again. Do these people have no sense? This is irritating. An intrusion into the normally peaceful end of my day. Usually just me, the channel, you, two larger islands, further, the dark outline of the distant peninsula guarding all. A rest from the daily battle of being *human*.

Now they're sitting to look around. All three of them. They don't know I'm watching. They don't know you know they are there.

Setting sun streaming pink beams through a rhomboid in the silver clouds just above the horizon where flows a translucent green river of sky. Above all that dense black cloud banked into the far west almost to the Antarctic, I like to think. No evening is ever the same as any previous one. Extraordinary.

They've stopped for a breather. Probably want to give up on the climb, but not one of them will dare to say it first. Conformity. Brings us to the brink of disaster, time and again. Handy though, for those who love to rule.

A launch passes through the channel, prow up. Such hubris. Look at me! Far to the south a yacht leans off the wind heading right at us.

They're on their way up again. A little more cautiously now that the beach is some distance below. Holding on to small branches. Looking up, thinking how far is it now, the top?

Rolling down, one is rolling down, over, and over, arms flailing out, legs skittering over the rocks, through the scrub. He's on the beach, he is not moving. Not moving.

Are his companions calling? They must be. Calling and listening. No movement, just the seagulls, whirling above, glaringly white in the angled light from the sun slipping below the horizon. The headland has swallowed the launch. Yacht tacking away.

Now what do I do.

I watch the other two edging down to their companion. I could ring 111. But I don't know. He could have a broken back. Or a sprained thumb. A series of post-event complaints come to mind, as reported in the local paper. "Some hysterical woman rang. Should have waited. We knew what we were doing. Helicopter came all the way for nothing. God's sake!" Or this. "We found out later some woman was watching us from her house. She saw the whole thing happen, and she did nothing. Nothing! Can you *believe* it? He would still be alive if she had called 111."

I cannot be responsible for the mistakes of others, surely. Compassion, yes. Oh look at that. His companions have reached him. He is sitting up. What a relief.

Now where were we? Ah yes, our daily communion. The sun's last rays shoot into the green sky. You were telling me something. Does it go like this: Tides work their unchanging rhythm. Day follows night follows day. Stay at the heart of things. Know your place. Is that close?

To purchase extra copies of Island Voices

by mail order -

Email ian@farmside.co.nz for order form and banking details.